The Center of Experience

A blueprint for creating the experience-led enterprise

SECOND EDITION

by Greg Kihlström

Published by:

Agile Brand, LLC

3100 Clarendon Boulevard #200

Arlington, VA 22201

www.theagilebrand.com

First Edition: December 2019

Second Edition: July 2023

The publisher is not responsible for websites (or their content) that are not owned by the publisher.

Edited by Janelle Kihlström

Cover Design by Alicia Recco

Illustrations by Greg Kihlström

ISBN – 979-8-85-120416-6

Contents

For Lindsey:

The experience of knowing you

continues to make my life better.

Acknowledgements

As with any work of its type, this book was produced with a lot of help from great people I continually rely on for good (and sometimes contrary) ideas, strength, and support.

There have been several people who have influenced the thoughts and ideas in this book, both the first and second editions. While an exhaustive list would be difficult to produce (and too long to print), a few of these include the team at Cravety, particularly Ed Bodensiek and JG Staal, the team at MotiveX, including Matt Johnson, the team at VMware, particularly Josh Olson, as well as The Office of Experience Team, including Carlos Manalo in particular, as well as many others.

Thanks to my sister Janelle for her editing support, and to Alicia Recco for her continued (and stellar) design work on the cover and for being such a good steward of my personal brand. Thanks also to the wonderful Diane Magers for contributing the Foreword to this book; it's great to have the support of such an expert in the field.

Others who have provided helpful ideas, insights, and support include Amy Christopher, Gail Legaspi-Gaull, Lisa Nirell, Josh Olson, Lou Pugliese, Claudia Silon, Patty Soltis, Mark Slatin, and Greg Melia of the CXPA.

As always, my wife Lindsey could not be more supportive or understanding of all my endeavors. This has been both an exciting and challenging year, and I could not have done any of it without her support.

To anyone not mentioned specifically, I apologize for doing so, but I will say that I am truly blessed to have even half the friends, colleagues, and family who support me like you have. I only hope I can return the support you've given me at some point.

"Life is not a problem to be solved,
but a reality to be experienced."

Søren Kierkegaard

Foreword

After spending years forging the exploding discipline of experience-led transformation and talking with experience professionals across the globe, I've discovered those in our burgeoning field often feel overwhelmed, alone on an island, fighting organizational obstacles and lacking a great blueprint for how we can really help our brands succeed.

It's not for a lack of effort; it is often a lack of thinking and acting as futurists. Futurists who see a vision and a different way of working, thinking and acting as a brand.

I've known Greg for several years. He is ahead of his time – pushing the boundaries of how we should think and act within organizations to really help brands gain traction in this crazy, changing world.

By creating The Center of Experience, Greg has given us a practical, value-driven blueprint for building experience skills, capabilities and competencies for a brand or organization. Experience management is often misunderstood, fuzzy, focused on tactics and scores and a "nice to have" program in organizations. In fact, it is a business discipline that establishes rigor and structure which provides a holistic foundation for the way an organization works to engage everyone – employees, customers, partners, and suppliers.

The author has created a step-by-step recipe for exploring the most critical assets of your organization - your customers and employees. He shares real situations and stories about how you can discover the interactions everyone in the ecosystem has with your brand.

You will find it is about creating knowledge and momentum from a different vantage point and, most importantly, about defining the steps to change how you approach our discipline in a different way.

As you read this impactful book, you will find yourself realizing your work is actually about personal and professional change for everyone in the organization. It reflects experience discipline as more human/personal and encourages the psychology of "why" – discussing motivation, impact, structure, personalization. You'll discover this powerful, holistic way to approach our discipline and profession by breaking from the typical data – action – metric cycle. It's all here. With honest expression and stimulating, provocative thinking, Greg comes from a place of passion and understanding of what it takes to achieve value. You'll be reading words from someone who has been there and done that. Who has a vision and a plan for the "how to" rather than just the theory.

Regardless of where you are in your journey, you will benefit from the insights, advice and tactical approach in *The Center of Experience*. Roll up your sleeves, gather change agents in your organization, use the steps in this book and achieve your vision!

There is no doubt this book is a labor of love and with a lens of the future. Greg has spent years partnering with organizations to build capabilities for them to discover and impact experiences and engagement with their customers.

How to tactically build a work/life experience really comes to life in *The Center of Experience.* Enjoy this succinct, impactful work and keep your planner handy – you'll need it for all the ideas you will generate to move your experience discipline forward!

Diane Magers, CCXP, MS, MBA
Former Interim CEO for the Customer Experience Professionals Association; Founder and CEO, Experience Catalysts

Preface to the Second Edition

As you are probably aware, a lot has happened since January 2020 and today (that was an intentional understatement!). A global pandemic that shifted the nature of many people's employee experience, a massive focus on digital innovation during that pandemic, economic shifts, global turmoil, and more have all changed many of the ways we look at business, customer, and employee experience.

That said, while there may be some statistics and anecdotes in this book that have held up better than others, the principles behind the Center of Experience remain true.

Thus, you may notice a few facts and figures that are a few years old, or some examples that may feel like they come from a pre-pandemic era. While I've endeavored to update many of these, I have left some intact where I felt they don't distract from the understanding and application of the core principles.

My goal in this book was to update it enough to focus more on practical applications and cut some of the elements that I felt distracted from the talk of implementing a fully functioning center of excellence around experience, or Center of Experience.

Thanks for going on this journey with me!

Introduction

I originally wanted to start this book with a perfect, yet very personal, example of what encapsulates great Experience with a capital "E". By that, I mean that summation of employee and customer experience that made me forever loyal to company x, or wanted to work until I retired for company y. Instead of finding that single perfect example, I could much more easily name countless examples of small cases where a small action, the design of a process or interface, or some other detail occurred and added up to either a positive or negative feeling about a company, product, or brand.

This thinking reflects reality, much more than a single grand gesture. Sure, in the movies, it's a grand gesture that turns the tide, or wins over the hardened heart. But here in the real world, brands live or die by a thousand little actions and gestures. If they wait for the opportunity to do a single grand one, it will likely be too late. Consumers have way too many choices, have ready access anywhere they are, and are too busy for such things. The battle for consumers' (and employees') hearts and minds is fought every day in countless ways. Thus, the value of a great experience needs to be woven through every plan, every action, every idea.

The Experience-Led Organization

The term "experience-led" is used in the subtitle of this book. To me, it means that an organization understands the importance of both employee and customer experience enough to *lead* its thinking and initiatives with the idea that if the experience is valuable and rewarding, the company will tangibly benefit.

Being experience-led comes with many challenges, since companies have not traditionally had "experience" departments, and also because experience itself spans so many disciplines and facets of a consumer's or employee's interactions with an organization. Many have awakened to this to varying degrees, as evidenced by Gartner's findings back in 2018 that "improving the employee experience" was one of HR's top three goals for 2019[1], as well as similar statistics for customer experience. More recently, PWC found that luxury customers are willing to pay a price premium of up to around 15% to receive great customer experience[2]. There is still much work to be done, and so I wrote this book because I see several gaps for organizations that want to tie both employee and customer experience together and become truly experience-led.

The Power of Experience

We find ourselves at an inflection point in the relationship between brands and their audiences, where customers and employees are demanding better and more valuable experiences. Companies must keep up with this demand in order to remain competitive. This includes competition for both customers as well as employees. More importantly, while many organizations have traditionally focused on external-facing initiatives first, it is the ones which start internally that have the greatest potential to provide long-term positive benefits. I believe strongly in this, and have dedicated much of my writing and my work with customers to work with them to improve the customer experience provided by their organizations.

Employee Experience (EX) and Customer Experience (CX) have the power to individually influence an organization for the better. Benefits from EX include improved productivity, engagement, and turn-over rates, among other changes. But combined, they have the power to truly transform. When these three elements are combined successfully, we refer to the phenomenon as brand experience.

For many organizations, enabling great experiences for employees and customers supported by process, organizational culture, technologies such as artificial intelligence and machine learning, and the ability to measure across the elements will be a game-changer. The speed at which these practices are applied could be the difference between exponential growth and losing out to the competition. However, as many early adopters have found, there are many hurdles to overcome for successful implementation of CX and EX within an organization.

Unfortunately, because EX and CX have unique requirements and are often applied by disconnected teams, this cannot be pinned down to a single issue. For improved experience to deliver upon its promise, a complex interworking of different factors will need to line up. These range from organizational and operational to the people, processes, and technologies utilized. Companies that understand how to make that work will be the winners, able to outsmart their competition.

For instance, in the 2019 edition annual CMO Survey by Deloitte, Duke University, and the American Marketing Association, the top challenge in managing customer experience was developing the necessary capabilities inside the organization to design, deliver, and monitor the customer experience[3].

To address this, I first shared the Center of Experience (COX) framework in 2020 to help organizations with all of the tools needed to enable great experiences for both employees and customers, and to achieve and measure the return on investment that is referred to as Return on Experience (RO_x). I'm excited to share this revised version, based on learnings and practical applications since that time and the writing of this second edition.

The flexibility of the Center of Experience framework is also an asset. While it contains all of the aspects needed to have a true brand experience, you do not have to adopt every piece of it if you have some of the pieces already established within your organization. Thus, you can think of this as either an entire platform to use, or as a resource that you can rely on to fill gaps in your current experience transformation.

This book provides the blueprint for you to create your own Center of Experience.

Who this book is for (and what this book is not)

This book is intended for experience practitioners who have the task of either setting up or improving the customer experience (CX) and/or employee experience (EX) within their organizations. As it can serve as a blueprint for your company, the Center of Experience framework, is made to be flexible to the needs of any organization, regardless of its experience maturity. You can take the pieces that are missing or relevant to you without having to adopt the entire model verbatim.

On the contrary, this book is not meant to convince the "uninitiated" that investing in customer experience and employee experience is a worthy endeavor. While I wholeheartedly believe that, there are many books dedicated to the value of EX and CX. Some valuable statistics and justification for approaches are given along the way, but this is first and foremost a working guide to creating a Center of Experience of your own.

What we're going to discuss

I've separated this book into three parts, with the following structure:

- **Part 1** provides us with a definition of the Center of Experience and provides both an explanation of the requirements as well as what it is intended to accomplish.
- **Part 2** discusses the six properties of the Center of Experience, and how each individual item is designed and measured for success.
- **Part 3** talks about the application of the Center of Experience, and some methods to implement it in your own organization.

Idea starters

Since the intent of this book is to be as prescriptive as possible of how to set up your own Center of Experience, there is only so much that a single book can share with a general audience. Because of this, I decided to include some "idea starters" at the end of most of the chapters that may help you find a way to personalize the ideas discussed, or to start a piece of the process. My hope is that this helps you create your own Center of Experience more easily.

Appendix 1: Glossary

Because I am mentioning several terms that are potentially new to at least some of the audiences of this book, and introducing a few to the vernacular, I've included a glossary in the back that you can refer to if you come across something that would be helpful to learn more about.

Appendix 2: Sample Experience Maturity Assessment

Since this is a practical guide to standing up your own Center of Experience, I wanted to provide a sample slimmed-down version of the experience maturity assessment that I have used with clients to determine where their starting point is, and how we can best help them.

All in all, this should provide you with the blueprint to set up your own Center of Experience. All right, let's get started!

Part 1:
Definition

In this first section, we're going to discuss what we mean by brand experience as a combination of customer and employee experience, and the purpose of the Center of Experience. We'll also discuss what the Center of Experience is intended to accomplish, and provide a high-level definition of the elements involved.

Let's get started with a definition of what is meant by *brand experience.*

1.1
Brand experience

Change is inevitable and often necessary for companies to survive. We live in a time when, if your industry has not already been "disrupted" by some new approach, it will be soon. This is so prevalent, in fact, that many companies aren't waiting for external disruptions and are enacting massive changes to themselves.

So, change is coming in many forms, and under many names. There is "digital transformation," sometimes shorthanded to just "transformation," along with other things like a move to substantial investments in data science and exponential technologies (often using artificial intelligence and machine learning). For many of us, "experience" is another one of these major game changers. Except that experience has always existed; it is just getting a new focus because of factors too numerous to do justice in this book. But, just as the big data craze (and its subsequent investments) of several years ago enabled a lot of the technology and digital transformation of today, there have been many factors that have contributed to the current *era of experience* such as the following (and many more):

- Greater consumer choice
- Lower unemployment rates
- Greater access to technology
- Greater access to data

Even if your brand is achieving success in many areas, there are always areas in which it can be improved. The premise of the Center of Experience is that motivated employees and leaders contribute to a healthy culture, which makes the desired change possible in order to yield tangible results like cost savings through reduced turnover, or increased revenue from customers who buy more, buy more often, and refer others who buy.

Motivation

It all starts with motivation. When employees are motivated to do great work, there is higher productivity and engagement, as well as higher retention rates. These all translate into tangible benefits for the organization.

Motivation and Culture

Keeping employees motivated allows an organization to pivot in the best strategic direction while staying unified. This translates into greater efficiency in accomplishing key strategic objectives.

Culture and Brand

An aligned culture creates a cohesive brand and value proposition for employees and customers. This translates to loyal customers who buy more, buy more often, and recommend others. This same brand works with employees and translates into further loyalty, referrals, and retention.

As we dive deep into the approaches and inner workings of the Center of Experience, or COX, it is important to start at the very beginning. The COX is based upon the foundation that a holistic brand experience provides tangible value to an organization.

Thus, we both start and end with the concept of a successful brand. This goes much deeper than the superficial things often associated with brands like logos and taglines. Instead, we look at brand and brand experience as every touchpoint a customer or employee has with an organization.

Defining Brand Experience

The definition of holistic experience within the center of experience is inclusive of both *customer* and *employee* experience, and achieving success with each individually is critical to achieving success with experience. This utilizes a definition of *brand experience* (BX) as the combination of both customer experience (CX) and employee experience (EX) (Figure 1.1).

This is illustrated as follows:

Brand Experience (BX) =

Employee Experience (EX) + Customer Experience (CX)

Thus, successful brand experience is the combination of successful employee experience and customer experience.

Expanding the definition of EX and CX

While in this book, I will refer broadly to internal experience as employee experience (or EX) and external experience as customer experience (or CX), I would be remiss if I didn't go into a little more detail here.

If we look at internal experience, this is more accurately split into two categories:

- Employees
- Leadership

I won't get into a lot of specific detail on the nuances of employees and leadership in this book, but it's important to keep in mind.

This can get even more complex depending on the type of organization. For instance, a university has students as well as employees, who could be seen as internal once they are accepted, since they often have access to systems and processes that a typical "customer" may not.

Likewise, with external experience, this can get even more complex. There are partners and vendors for many companies, or a trade or other membership association may have members. Thus, there might be more than one category for "customer" in your CX strategy and designs.

How CX and EX Work together

Successful companies have always understood that happy customers buy more, and buy more often. They also understand that happy employees stay longer (which costs a company less money over time), and contribute to happier customers.

This means that customer experience (CX) and employee experience (EX) have a lot to do with one another. Let's explore three ways that customer experience and employee experience intersect and can work together.

1: Feedback is best when timely and relevant

What's key here is making sure that employees get to see customer feedback where and when they can take the most action. This means having the tools and methods to listen for both internal and external feedback, as well as having the processes and discipline to review and respond.

Listening to customer feedback is critical to understanding both what they love as well as what they wish were improved. But it's not enough to simply listen. You need systems and processes in place to not only collect the information but do something meaningful with it. When I work with brands, I make sure to understand what silos or bottlenecks might be getting in the way of the right information getting to the best place.

When you actively listen to employee feedback, it empowers employees to be able to make the types of changes in the organization that keep them both productive and happy, which can lower attrition. The best part of this is that companies with satisfied employees often have an easier time creating satisfied customers.

2: Both customers and employees love feedback

One point of commonality between both happy employees and loyal customers is that they feel valued and rewarded, and receive feedback based on their actions. Whether this is through personalized customer experiences or meaningful recognition at the employee level, both are valued and valuable to an organization.

In fact, this is a case where the methods and tactics used to reward each group (customers and employees) will vary greatly, but the fact remains that employees who feel valued contribute to making customers who feel valued.

It is also important to understand that the same kind of incentives, rewards, and opportunities don't make all your employees more engaged or happier in their jobs. Make sure to keep in mind that everyone is different and is motivated by different things. When I work with a client on CX or EX (or both), I always make sure to emphasize that successful implementation isn't a one-size-fits-all approach. You need to make sure to account for a variety of tastes and motivators.

We will discuss motivation, both extrinsic and intrinsic, much more in a few chapters.

3: Experience is everything, and everything is experience

Let's end with perhaps the most obvious, but also the most inclusive tie-in between employee and customer experience. Not only is experience worth a lot to both employees and customers, both audiences consider experience to be a combination of *everything* they experience.

This means that focusing on having a really good experience part of the time, or on a few channels isn't enough. Your customers have grown device-agnostic and rarely use a single device to communicate with you. They don't care that your website gives a phenomenal user experience, if they try to call someone on the phone and are treated rudely.

The same goes with employees. The employee experience starts from before their first day and extends throughout their employment, including their last day at work. Companies that embrace CX and EX understand that the details matter, and that every moment helps make up an overall experience. The results speak for themselves. Companies with highly engaged employees outperform their competitors by 147%, according to Gallup[4], yet according to Gallup's 2022 State of the Workplace report, 85% of employees are either unengaged or actively disengaged[5]. Whether it is quiet quitting, bare-minimum Mondays, working multiple jobs, or any other variation, the challenge to companies is to find that way to engage employees.

Understanding the important link between customer experience and employee experience can give brands an important competitive advantage in a crowded marketplace, particularly when over three quarters of companies are already competing primarily on the basis of *customer experience*[6]. Focusing on both ends of the experience (customer and employee) is a win-win for all, whether the job market is good or bad for employers or employees.

Idea Starters

1. One important mind shift is to stop thinking about a *customer* brand and an *employee* brand as simply being related to one another. It's time to start thinking of them as one and the same. Remember, employees are consumers when they leave work (and even sometimes while still at work).

2. Another mind shift is the move away from deeming a tactic successful without understanding its effect on the rest of the experience. A simple example from the world of marketing is this: you can spend a lot of money on advertising which generates a lot of traffic. So, from one perspective, you can report to your CMO that you drove 120% more traffic to a landing page last month than the previous month. However, if you look at the *quality* of the traffic and find out that 99% of those people failed to take an action, you'll soon realize you

just wasted a lot of money. The same applies to experience. Getting high satisfaction ratings at a single stage in a journey is good, but unless it follows through the experience, and results in desired actions being taken, it's no different than the expensive but unsuccessful advertising campaign.

1.2
The Rationale for the Center of Experience

Both customer experience (CX) and employee experience (EX) are growing in their importance within organizations today, and in order to keep up, many teams and disciplines must be aligned in order to address this wide-reaching practice area. CX is so important, in fact, that according to a 2017 Gartner survey, 66% of businesses say they compete primarily based on customer experience[7], and that number continues to increase.

Companies will often set up a center of excellence that is built around a capability or area of practice. While this can be a physical place as well, it is best to think of it as a virtual collection of people, processes, and technology that are aligned around a specific area of practice. For instance, in the realm of artificial intelligence, Deloitte reports that as of late 2018, 37% of enterprises surveyed had set up an

AI center of excellence[8], and with the recent hype about AI as of the end of 2022 and beginning of 2023, that number has only grown. A center of excellence that focuses on experience (both customers and employees) can be a benefit to any organization that adopts it. I refer to this as a "Center of Experience," and thus the title of this book was born!

The alignment between customer experience and employee experience is critical. A 2017 Qualtrics study showed that 79% of employees at companies with above-average customer experience are highly engaged in their jobs, compared to less than half at companies with average or below-average customer experience scores[9].

When we create a Center of Experience, it contains measurements and processes to optimize the following elements to provide a holistic view of experience:

- **Internal and external teams** involved in both employee and customer experience
- **Organizational culture** diagnostics and processes to enable culture change where needed, and an alignment on a customer-centered culture
- **Branding** for internal and external communications
- **Governance** processes and practices to ensure consistency and compliance
- **Data components,** including customer and employee data, plus data science components, including artificial intelligence and machine learning

- **Environments**, including both physical ones such as office space for employees or retail spaces for customers, as well as virtual ones for each
- **Measurements**, including a maturity model that shows how advanced the organization is in its experience practices, as well as analytics that measure customer and employee experience
- **Platforms** to support experience initiatives for customers and employees

These eight elements comprise an organization's entire experience ecosystem for both internal (employees) and external (customers) audiences. Let's now discuss why the format of the Center of Experience works, with three main points.

Reason 1: Centralizes experience within an organization

A common CX pitfall is making customers feel as if an organization is disconnected or disorganized, causing them frustration by having to repeat themselves to different people, log into separate systems to manage different parts of their account, or receive inconsistent products and services during their relationship with a brand. Employees often have different challenges, but many stem from a lack of cohesion within an organization.

A Center of Experience creates a common "operating system" within the company that aligns everyone around providing consistent, excellent experiences for all audiences. This includes leadership,

GREG KIHLSTRÖM | 34

employees, and even partners or vendors. By breaking down traditional silos between departments such as marketing, HR, operations, and technology, employees and customers alike feel the difference when everyone is using the same playbook.

Reason 2: Ties employee experience and customer experience together

Happy customers buy more, they buy more *often,* and they refer other customers more often as well—you'll hear me say that a lot in this book, and anywhere I speak or write! The way you create happy customers is by creating happy employees first. This means that the closer you can tie your employee experience efforts and your customer experience efforts, the more successful you will be. A Center of Experience helps to build this synergy between CX and EX, and makes it part of the company culture.

For instance, a former client in the B2B space recently set up a customer experience certification program. This program, which was created to ultimately target and improve their CX efforts, demonstrates closely how a happier employee enabled to do great work is able to deliver better customer service, improving their experience and positively impacting the bottom line through longer relationship and often larger sales. Employee experience and customer experience are so closely tied through a Center of Experience that it makes sense to strategically align them in this way.

Reason 3: Experience measurement and goals are centralized and accountable

Finally, the critical area of measuring and showing results of investments in improving both customer and employee experience is streamlined by creating a Center of Experience. It can be incredibly challenging to align metrics that are pulled from across an enterprise. If, however, the Center of Experience is created with measurement and optimization in mind from the start, the right numbers will be built into the processes and integrated into the reporting without the need to cobble together reports from disparate sources.

There are practical benefits from this deeper integration between CX and EX as well. This includes designing and creating common dashboard interfaces that pull in data and information from across the enterprise. The Center of Experience then becomes the central hub of these important metrics that are increasingly becoming critical to business success.

It's not enough to simply say that you are either customer-focused or employee-focused, or both. While communication is key to any effort involving your key audiences, establishing a true Center of Experience means that you are backing up your messaging with the infrastructure and support that a truly experience-led organization possesses.

Thus, the Center of Experience is depicted as a wheel (Figure 1.2) with a customer-centric culture at its core, but tightly integrating all things EX and CX together in order to ensure success under the umbrella of "Brand Experience" as mentioned earlier in the book.

Defining the Center of Experience

Figure 1.2: The Center of Experience

The Center of Experience (COX) consists of 4 components that work in coordination with one another:

- **Component 1: Brand Experience Framework**
  This is the underlying methodology of how experience is defined, designed, and measured

- **Component 2: Customer-Centric Culture**

  This includes the underlying engine that powers the framework: intrinsic motivation of human beings

- **Component 3: Internal and External Audiences**

  This includes the people and groups that will implement the framework utilizing the processes, tools, and methods within the Center

- **Component 4: 6 Properties of the COX**

  This includes the processes, tools and methods that are created and optimized in order to grow the Center of Experience:

  - Brand
  - Governance
  - Data
  - Environment
  - Measurement
  - Platform

We'll discuss each of the components of the Center of Experience in detail in the chapters that follow.

1.3
Component 1: Brand Experience Framework

Let's revisit the Brand Experience formula (Figure 1.3) from the previous chapter:

Brand Experience (BX) =

Employee Experience (EX) + Customer Experience (CX)

Here, we clearly see that a great brand experience is made up of a great employee experience and a great customer experience. Without both working together, true success is not possible. To define and measure success with any type of experience, we first need to understand what we mean by "experience."

Defining Experience

To go a little deeper, let's now look at how we even define the word *experience*.

This can be briefly described by saying the following: experience is the combination of people, places, platform, and the actions audiences take, which consist of both customers and employees.

The 4 categories and 10 elements of experience

There is a lot of nuance, then, to experience, especially since we need to split up our definition of it into four pieces. There's a good reason for this: just as our experiences aren't one-dimensional, creating them can't only take one dimension into account.

These 4 main categories (Figure 1.6) of experience consist of 10 individual elements, as illustrated in the diagram below:

Figure 1.6: The 10 Elements of Experience

They all work together to form a cohesive customer or employee experience. Let's explore each of the 10 elements of experience that fall within those 4 main categories.

People

These are the actors participating in journeys, actions, and managing the processes and platforms, and within this element, we have two subcategories:

- **Cohesion**

   The way experience initiatives are embedded and integrated in the organizational structure

- **Culture**

   The explicit and implicit behaviors and expectations that shape the workforce, as well as the consumers that support the brand

Places

These are the physical and virtual spaces where experience occurs, and they include a single element within the Center of Experience:

- **Environment**

   Physical places and virtual spaces where employees and/or customers interact with one another

Platform

This consists of the journeys, processes and technology that are utilized to facilitate great experiences. It includes 4 sub-categories:

- **Process**

   Consistency and sophistication of methods and tools used in order to provide great customer and employee experience

- **Intelligence**

   How analytics, data science, and artificial intelligence are used throughout the customer and employee experience

- **Technology**

   The tools, platforms, and infrastructure that support experience for internal and external audiences

- **Compliance**

  The way that risk is managed, and regulations are followed and enforced, as well as the way that rules and processes are maintained and improved

Action

This refers to the measurable activities performed across the people, places, and platforms created to enable experiences, and contains three sub-categories:

- **Results**

  The way that success with experience is measured

- **Strategy**

  The goals and principles that guide an experience-led organization

- **Ideation**

  The process to identify, plan, and socialize experience initiatives that provide business impact and ROI

Idea Starter

To get started, begin to delineate between the people, places, and actions that make up your customer and employee experience. While a successful brand experience relies on all of these pieces working well together, it's important to optimize each one and begin to understand how each works together.

1.4
Component 2: Customer-Centric Culture

Culture is something that is unique to an organization, the time and place it occupies, and the people that belong to it. Because of all of these factors, one could say that each organizational culture is unique and distinct. Never has this been more important, whether we are talking about great leadership or an engaged, motivated workforce. Or as Dr. Jennifer Chatman, professor of management at UC Berkeley-Haas says, "Culture is your strategy execution engine. I encourage leaders to define their strategy first, and once those strategic aspirations are defined, then think clearly about the most important behaviors and values that are going to enable the company to achieve its strategic objectives.[10]"

What do we mean by "customer-centric?"

While I go into much greater detail about what we mean by a customer-centric culture in my more recent book, House of the Customer, let me paraphrase here.

As you might guess, a customer-centric culture is one that asserts that what is right for the customer will translate into the long-term best outcome for the company. This means that the needs of the customer are taken into primary consideration when planning.

At first glance, you would be hard-pressed to find a brand or executive who disagrees with this. However, when it comes to making the necessary decisions, investments, and prioritizations, some organizations clearly practice what they preach, while others stay beholden to short-term, reactionary decisions.

Brands that are truly customer-first put their resources into building customer relationships. This is sometimes at the expense of short-term gains, but always with the understanding that investing in improving the customer experience is key. Coincidentally, most category leaders are defined by a distinct customer experience and loyal consumer relationships.

Customer-centric thus means that when decisions are made, resources are allocated, or strategies are weighed, the relationship with and considerations of their customers are a primary determiner. Although the customers are certainly not the only consideration, they also are not an afterthought when considering profits, shareholder value, or other important factors.

What is a healthy culture?

There are tangible benefits to a healthy organizational culture. While there are a wide variety of statistics on the topic, a recent study by Oxford Economic and Grant Thornton[11] pegged a difference of 56% between turnover at organizations with a healthy versus unhealthy culture (Figure 2.2).

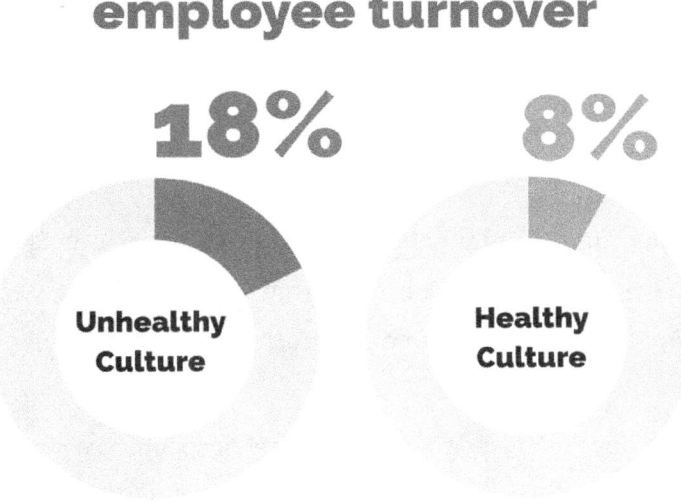

Figure 2.2: Employee turnover in unhealthy versus healthy cultures

Culture also extends to external perceptions and customer behavior. For instance, 87% of customers' positive sentiment about Starbucks has to do with the way they treat their employees[12]. That's pretty powerful, and a win-win if you ask me. Not only has the company committed to supporting the employee experience, but it is netting tangible results because of it.

The Center of Experience includes an organizational culture assessment that is based on a longstanding framework, the Competing Values Framework, which itself is backed by decades of research and validation[13]. The COX has added to this original framework by looking at additional elements we know are vital to any organization that will be successful in an environment of continual change and disruption. These additions also have proven return on investment indexes that create additional value in the assessment of organizational culture.

Why is culture so important?

Why is it important that an organization define and measure its culture? We believe that culture is an operating system for how work gets done. Approached as a common platform, when successfully managed, it accomplishes the following:

- Determines how leaders *lead* and how decisions are made
- Determines the way that employees interact with each other
- Promotes cooperation with one another towards a shared goal over detrimental competition
- Guides employees with a sense of direction
- Helps employees understand the brand of the company they work for, far better than any "branding" campaign
- Unites diverse people under a shared purpose
- Promotes healthy relationships and dynamics in the workplace

- Allows employees "psychological safety" to put in their best work

While we can all agree that organizational culture health is important, it is often difficult for many within an organization to truly understand when there are issues, and what those issues might be.

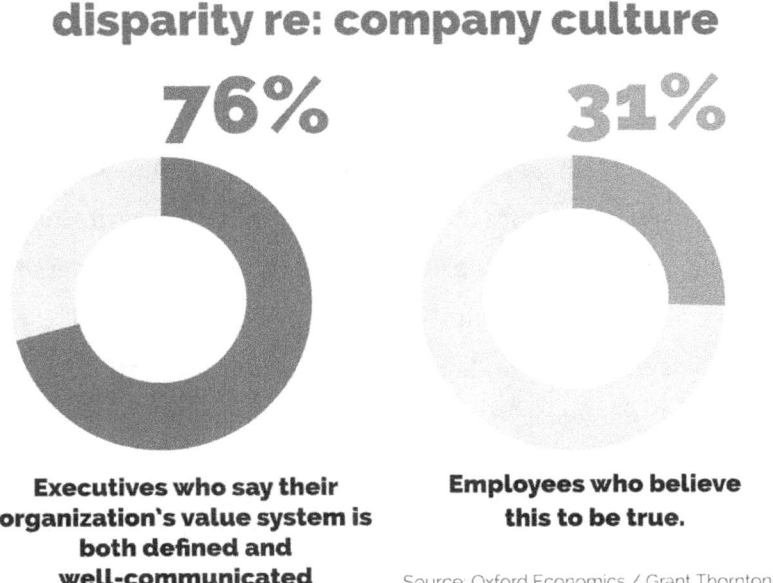

disparity re: company culture

76%

Executives who say their organization's value system is both defined and well-communicated

31%

Employees who believe this to be true.

Source: Oxford Economics / Grant Thornton

Figure 2.3: The disparity between executives and employees regarding company culture.

As part of the Grant Thornton and Oxford Economics study I referenced earlier, it was noted that while over three-quarters of executives say their organization has a well-defined value system (Figure 2.3), less than one-third of employees believe it to be true[14].

On the pages that follow, we have outlined our approach, the measurements included, and how to use the framework.

Background

The organizational culture methodology within the Center of Experience is founded upon the well-researched and documented Competing Values Framework (CVF). This framework provides decades of substantiation and a wealth of peer-reviewed validation.

Initially developed through research done by faculty members of the University of Michigan[15], the Competing Values Framework describes the major indicators of effective organizational performance. Its applications are wide-ranging, from creating theories of leadership effectiveness, organizational culture and design, and even brain functioning. As such, CVF is understood to be one of the most important such frameworks in the history of business.

CVF describes two primary dimensions:
1. Flexibility vs. stability
2. Collaboration vs. competition

No point along these two dimensions is understood as "good" or "bad" as different organizations have different needs. They are, as the name would suggest, competing priorities and no organization can be equally both at the same time.

Thus, the framework adopts the quadrant format which allows an organization to plot its current point at any given point in time within the appropriate place.

It is upon this research-based and time-tested framework that the culture piece of the Center of Experience was built. With CVF as its foundation, we have added several components that provide additional insights and value, which we will discuss in this document.

The organizational culture quadrant

Since no organization's culture is wholly comprised of a single element, the framework instead uses a quadrant model, which allows a dominant culture, but allows for of diversity, which we will see later is a critical component to successful culture.

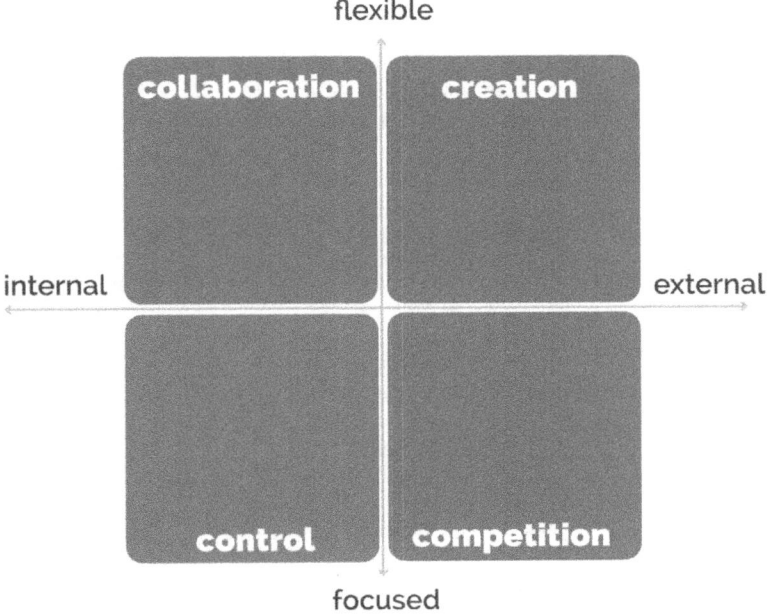

Figure 2.4: The organizational culture quadrant

Based on the Competing Values Framework's four archetypes (CVF uses different names, but each quadrant shares the same overall characteristics), we have labeled these as the following:

1. Collaboration
2. Control
3. Creation
4. Competition

Every organization has some aspect of each of these characteristics within it. Thus, measuring an organizational culture map never pinpoints a culture within only one quadrant (Figure 2.5). Instead, it is mapped like the following:

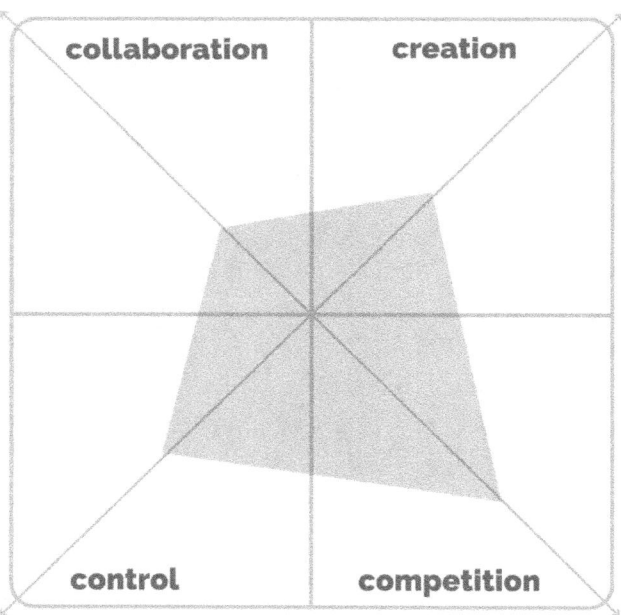

Figure 2.5: How an organizational culture maps on the quadrants

Let's now review definitions of each of the archetypes that comprise the organizational culture quadrant.

The four archetypes and the organizational culture quadrant

Collaboration

In a dominant culture of collaboration, a tribal or teamwork-based way of interacting is central to the organization16. This means that team members are more involved in the decision-making process.

This particularly contrasts with a competition culture, where there is more individualism and there can be a tendency towards siloed decision-making. The collaboration-dominant culture is also a lot more inward-focused where changes and improvements tend to be based on what will make the organization perform better for its employees.

Leaders in the collaboration quadrant are often thought of as facilitators, mentors, or team builders. They enable teams to do great work.

The benefits of this type of culture are that people are highly valued, and often leadership is grown from within, and generally speaking the organization is focused on long-term growth and goals. Drawbacks can include slower outcomes, and lack of focus, with more of a "country club" feel than that of a growing company.

Creation

In a dominant culture of creation, innovation is central to the organization and how it functions[17]. In this type of company, rapid ideation and change is emphasized, along with specialization of skillsets.

Unlike the collaboration culture, the creation culture does feature teamwork when focused on a specific project or outcome, but those teams then disband when the task is completed. In this way, collaboration is necessary to innovate, but not a systemic part of everyday work. In other research this has been described as ambiguity culture[18], where there are less rigid processes and rules, as compared to the control-dominant culture.

That being said, a creation-dominant culture does not necessarily lack defined processes, as long as it is able to transcend them when innovation demands it.

Leaders in a create culture are innovators, visionaries, and entrepreneurs. They have bold plans and need motivated teams to follow them in doing new things.

The benefits of a create culture are that they are often able to frequently create innovative, breakthrough ideas, and are able to focus on the long-term growth of the organization. Drawbacks include a sometimes-chaotic environment where radical ideas are prone to either wild success or costly failures, as well as goals that are difficult to achieve.

Control

In a dominant culture of control, there is a focus on organization and hierarchy.19 Efficiency, repeatability, and process are central to the priorities of the company.

This contrasts directly with the creation dominant culture, where the employee is generally given more latitude to circumvent established methods and processes for the sake of innovation and trailblazing new ideas.

Leaders of control-dominant cultures are organizers, monitors, and coordinators. They make sure the company is a well-oiled machine. Efficiency, timeliness, and consistency are valued above many other things.

Advantages of this type of dominant culture are a consistent set of incremental improvements that include higher quality, greater productivity, and more profits. Drawbacks can include an overly bureaucratic organization that shuns radical ideas in favor of pragmatic ones, to the detriment of innovation.

Competition

In a dominant culture of competition, the emphasis is less internal than it is external. This keeps the organization focused on winning by gaining competitive advantage in the marketplace.

This culture needs both order and innovation in order to remain competitive in the long-term, sometimes oscillating between the two, even as competition remains the dominant archetype.

It is on the other end of the spectrum from the collaboration-dominant culture, with the contrast being that in a competition culture, there is less sustained teamwork and more singular decision-making.

Leaders in the competition quadrant are producers themselves and drive their team members hard to achieve goals. The values that drive them are increasing market share, achieving goals, and greater profitability.

Advantages of the competition-dominant culture are a very customer-centric view of goals and initiatives (since happy customers equal more sales). There is also more organization and planning as opposed to the creation and collaboration cultures.

Drawbacks include the possibility of an extreme competition-focused culture feeling like a sweat shop, or filled with people engaging in unsustainable behaviors that are short-term focused.

The two axes of flexibility and focus

As we discussed above, there are two pairs of dominant culture attributes that are at either ends of a spectrum, which we are referring to as the two axes of flexibility and focus.

- Collaboration / Competition
- Creation / Control

Let's now look at the two axes that intersect the four archetypes of organizational culture.

Flexibility/Rigidity

These refer to how much process is followed and enforced, as well as how free employees feel to work outside of established guidelines in order to be successful in achieving company objectives.

Internal/External Focus

In addition to flexibility and rigidity, there is also the aspect of the internal versus external focus of the organizational culture.

Measuring organizational culture

Now that we've established definitions within the framework, we can discuss how a company measures itself against the organizational culture quadrant.

Assessing the Gap: Seven Measurements of Culture

The culture framework in the Center of Experience includes an assessment that allows an organization to measure several things:

- its location along the organizational culture quadrant
- the gap between employee expectation and reality as well as leadership expectations of the 10 elements of culture outlined below

Let's explore the seven measurements of culture:

Development

This defines how an organization nurtures and grows its employees throughout the employee journey. It also defines how an organization allocates time, money, property, and other assets to support its team.

Purpose

This defines why an organization prioritizes certain values, activities, and measurements and its reason for existing. It is also how an organization prioritizes, plans, and identifies both challenges and opportunities.

Diversity

This defines and measures how an organization embraces people, ideas and solutions with varying perspectives and backgrounds. Companies that embrace diversity and inclusion have a broader pool of perspectives with which to innovate.

This is such a critical and historically overlooked aspect of successful corporate culture that it is hard not to underscore its importance. Because of this, diversity and inclusion is also included in our measurements of a successful culture.

It is critical that organizations actively look for ways to solve diversity and inclusion shortcomings. For example, women at Baker McKenzie, a global law firm, comprised 52% of the workforce yet only 23% of the firm's partners. After surveying and analyzing why, it turns out that many women didn't want to be partner as much as their male counterparts. However, by providing some more flexibility around remote working, better access to high-profile engagements, and a few other things, they were able to increase the number of women promoted to partner by 40% by 2018[20].

The first thing to keep in mind is that there is a difference between demographic diversity, and organizational culture diversity. Differences in demographics like ethnic background, gender, and socio-political ideals brings strength to an organization and should be embraced. A wide gap between ideal and perceived organizational culture, however, is not good, and can cause lack of alignment on approach, and even what success looks like.

There can also be a healthy variation in culture within different teams of an organization. While alignment is key to success, a little variation is to be expected. For instance, let's use the example of the collaboration-dominant culture. While that may be the ideal culture for many individuals, if everyone in the entire company was first and foremost a collaborator, there would be a lot of teamwork and a family atmosphere, which would be good. But there would be little to no external focus on the competition, and innovation would only occur to serve the internal needs of team members. Over time, the company would be overtaken by more aggressive competitors and for all the internal comradery, the organization would inevitably falter due to its solely inward focus.

Environment

This defines the quality of physical and virtual environments, and how technology is provided and supported for employees. The Center of Experience also looks at physical and virtual environments as a component to focus on.

Community

This defines how workplace behaviors such as meetings, process, and project management are handled and improved. If you don't find a way for your organization to run efficient meetings, for instance, you are losing productivity, and it often affects employee morale. The author Dave Barry once said, "If you had to identify, in one word, the reason why the human race has not achieved, and never will achieve, its full potential, that word would be 'meetings.'"

A Microsoft study back in 2005 found that employees said 71% of their meetings were considered "unproductive," that is, they didn't have a clear objective, nor did they find a clear set of next steps[21]. Considering there are over 11 million meetings per day in the United States alone[22], finding a way to be effective and efficient with projects, meetings and other communications is a constant struggle for many businesses, but finding success is key.

Alignment

This measures two very important things:

- What employee's expectations and desires are compared to what the organization is in reality, along with leadership's desired goals. We'll discuss this in more detail in a little bit when we talk about the "culture gap."

- The other aspect of alignment might also be referred to as "strength." This refers to how closely aligned team members within an organization are within the four quadrants. See the diagram below (Figure 2.6) and how the culture mapping on the left is very wide and spread out, showing that there is a lot of variation between teams. By contrast, the diagram on the right shows that the teams are much more tightly aligned along the "creation" and "competition" quadrants.

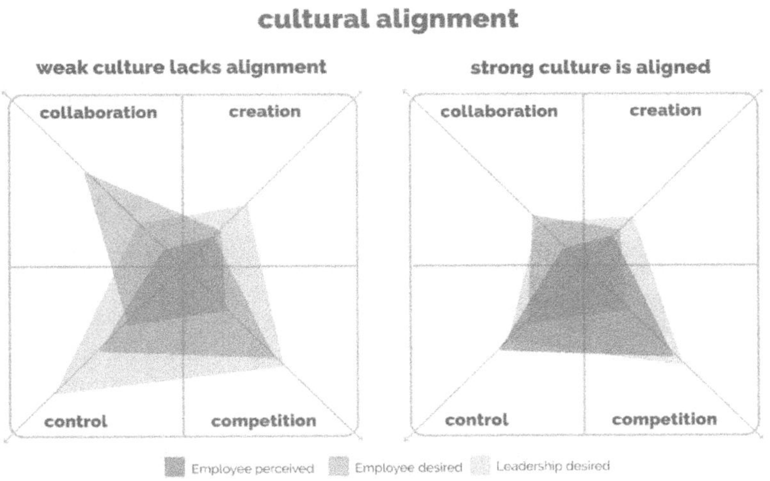

Figure 2.6: Weak and strong cultural alignment as mapped on the culture quadrant

Motivation

For an organization to influence its employees to assist with a cultural transition, the individual team members must be engaged and motivated to do so. This is where we need to understand the difference between intrinsic and extrinsic motivation.

To understand the true power of *intrinsic* motivators, we need to understand the difference between them and *extrinsic* motivators.

Extrinsic motivation refers to performing an action or behavior to receive an external reward or outcome. When individuals are extrinsically motivated to do something, they aren't concerned with whether the action is enjoyable or fulfilling. Instead, they are most concerned with the outcomes, whether performing an action to get rewarded or avoiding certain behaviors or actions to avoid punitive outcomes.

Intrinsic motivation is defined as performing an action or behavior because you enjoy the activity itself. This is motivation that comes from inside the performer (inherent behavior). Inspiration for acting on intrinsic motivation can be found in the action itself and not some form of external rewards.

Extrinsic motivators (such as salary increases and other perks), can work to an extent but their effectiveness diminishes over time, what has been referred to as the "hedonic treadmill.[23]" By contrast, intrinsic motivators have a more lasting effect, and have a deeper connection to the individual.

Everyone is influenced by some combination of several motivational factors that include things like the following:

- The desire to learn new things

- The desire to help or mentor others
- The desire to do new or innovative things
- The desire for autonomy over *how* they do their work

The above are just a few, but you can see that all of them have little to nothing to do with extrinsic or financial incentives or rewards. By using intrinsic motivators to engage employees, leadership can create a win-win situation: employees are satisfied in their jobs, and the organizational culture shifts to where it needs to be in order to move the company forward.

Results of the assessment and the culture gap

Once the assessment is completed, there are several valuable insights that can be gleaned.

Desired culture

This is a description of what an individual employee would like their workplace's culture to be like. While it may be thought of as their absolute ideal in some cases, the assessment usually brings out a healthy measure of realism in framing desired culture in terms of the specific company they work for.

This is not only helpful to understand about an individual and where within an organization they might fit best, but also when used in the aggregate it helps leadership understand the gap between what employees want and what the company is delivering.

Perceived culture

Unlike what an employee wishes the company they work for would be like, perceived culture is a description of their actual experience at the organization. This is a personal, subjective view of the organization and varies by individual, but when taken in the aggregate provides a realistic view of culture at the organization.

Leadership's desired culture

In addition to the two results of the assessment as described above, there is also a very important aspect that needs to be considered. While it is important to understand how employees perceive the organization and the delta between their expectations and what is delivered, it is also important that a company's leadership can set goals for the culture.

Thus, leadership's desired culture must be assessed and determined and measured against employees' desired and perceived culture.

Mapping the desired and perceived cultures

The process of mapping what both leadership and employees desire, as well as what employees currently perceive, provides us with a map like the one below:

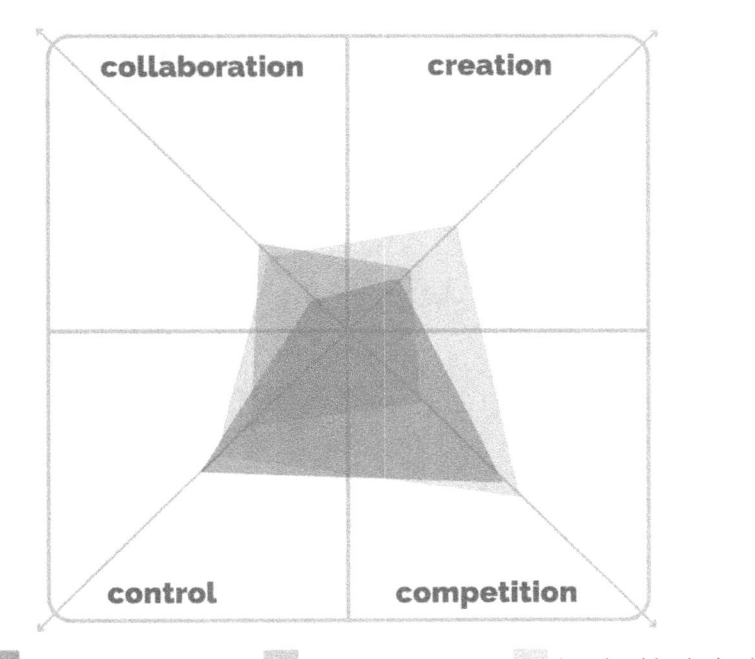

Figure 2.7: Mapping perceived and desired cultures onto the culture quadrant

You can see from viewing this that the leadership desires a more innovative yet market-driven culture, while employees perceive the organization as very control and process-oriented (the opposing value in our quadrants to creation and innovation).

Thus, from reading this chart, we can perceive a culture gap. Closing this gap should be the focus of the organizational culture work.

Culture gap

As I said above, the two results of both perceived and desired culture from employees are mixed with a third and very important aspect: leadership's desired culture. Below is a simplified version (Figure 2.8) that shows the center points of the polygons we saw above.

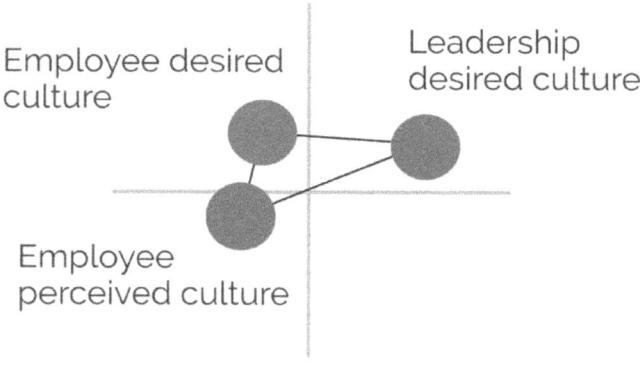

Figure 2.8: The culture gap

This is what is referred to as the "culture gap." Closing this gap leads to more strategic alignment across the organization and creates a less ambiguous culture overall. This lack of ambiguity allows an organization to hire the best people, create the most effective teams, and it allows potential new employees to better understand the company they are about to join.

A company's culture is not right or wrong

As we discussed the four types of cultures earlier in this chapter, you have seen the differences and the strengths and weaknesses of each. But it is important to note that there is no wrong or right type of culture. The culture needed in an organization is based on so many factors unique to its maturity, size, industry, external competition, and more, that it is impossible to say that one is good or bad.

Instead, we evaluate how successful a culture is in helping leaders achieve organizational priorities, and in helping employees have productive and satisfying careers while with the organization. The former is measurable against traditional scales such as revenue and profitability, and sales growth. The latter is measurable through employee net promoter score (eNPS) and employee retention.

Despite there not being a right or wrong type of culture, we do, however, see three primary areas in which to determine if a culture is successful or not.

Benefits of measuring culture

It goes without saying that there are real, tangible benefits to designing and fostering a successful organizational culture. But even the process of measurement can have multiple benefits and can be used in several practical applications. Let's discuss a few below.

Recruiting the best talent

Companies that actively understand both their current and desired cultures have a unique advantage when recruiting new employees. By understanding an individual's desired organizational culture and comparing that to both the current perceived culture as well as leadership's desired culture, a hiring manager can make informed decisions that set both the employee and the company up for success instead of a hiring mismatch.

Organizing teams

Similar to finding new talent from outside the organization, defining the desired organizational culture helps a company organize teams more successfully. Keep in mind that different teams within an organization might have different dominant cultures than others. This is not only to be expected, but is often optimal. It is more important that teams are growing or changing in the same trajectory as one another than that they map to the exact point in the culture quadrant.

Achieving organizational priorities

According to Gallup's 2017 State of the American Workforce report, 21% of employees strongly agree their performance is managed in a way that motivates them to do outstanding work, and only 33% of U.S. employees are actively engaged at work[24]. What's more, Gallup's 2023 report showed that only 23% are engaged at work, so we've seen a significant decline since the pandemic in that regard[25].

Organizations that can successfully define their ideal culture, match employees with that culture, and motivate the workforce to support their transition from their current to ideal culture will have a more motivated workforce because expectation and reality are more closely aligned.

Growing and maintaining a successful culture

While it may appear to be a matter of luck or happenstance to outside observers, a successful organizational culture takes a lot of intention and a concerted effort to implement and maintain. Let's explore some of the components of a successful culture.

Dominant culture vs. monolithic culture

An entire company isn't going to be completely one type of culture, though it will likely occupy a place within one of the quadrants as opposed to sitting square in the middle of both axes.

For this reason, we qualify the term culture by describing an organization's dominant culture, since the notion of a single, monolithic culture is both not desired, and unlikely in the first place. This particularly comes into play during the next point about diversity.

Importance of diversity

This is such a critical and historically overlooked aspect of successful corporate culture that it is hard not to underscore its importance. Because of this, diversity and inclusion is also included in our measurements of culture. An enterprise can simply not be truly successful without diversity and inclusion.

It is also important to make the distinction between diversity in culture, background and ideas, as opposed to diversity of purpose and goals. While the former is invaluable to an organization, the latter is more complicated.

In other words, companies benefit greatly from employing people with different ideas, socio-economic, cultural, and other types of backgrounds. What makes a strong culture is alignment around achieving a common purpose or goals for the company. When people (diverse or otherwise) are working towards different purposes or not aligned on mission, then an organization may be in need of alignment.

Shifting needs

In addition to the need for some types of diversity within an organization at any point in time, different types of cultures can often be needed or beneficial at different times in a company's lifespan.

For instance, think about what it takes to make a startup successful, versus a mature organization. Then, as that mature organization becomes challenged by disruptors and other upstarts, its needs change as well. There are times and places for more and less flexibility, as well as more of an innovative versus competitive culture throughout any organization's existence.

Smart leadership understands how to balance this so that, in addition to a general amount of diversity, the right emphasis is placed at the right times in the company's lifespan. Having tools like the Organizational Culture Assessment within the Center of Experience help this measurement and provide a dashboard that leaders can use to steer their dominant cultures in the most beneficial direction.

How to achieve culture change

We have already stated that a particular culture definition is not good or bad, only more successful or less successful in achieving its goals. There are times, however, when an organization needs to evolve from one dominant type of culture to another.

According to Hotjar's "State of Customer Experience 2019," of companies that considered themselves "mature" on the CX maturity scale, 41% of them considered themselves "customer-centric," while only 17% of the "least mature" respondents agreed.[26]

This brings us back to a key concept of the foundation of our Center of Experience: a customer-centric culture, which involves motivation and reward.

Motivation and Reward

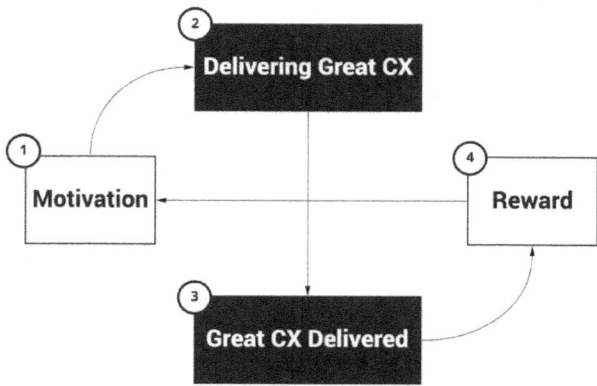

Figure 1.4.2, Motivation and Reward in the Customer-Centric Culture

The idea illustrated in Figure 1.4.2 is that when delivering a great customer experience becomes a motivating factor, it becomes its own reward. This goes along with the premise that employees don't derive all their motivation from extrinsic rewards like salary, bonuses, or other perks. Instead, a good part of their motivation comes from intrinsic motivations—that is, feelings of purpose and fulfillment within their job.

Evolution of organizational culture needs

Is there a single archetype that fits an organization over its lifetime? While that may be the case for a handful of companies, what is more likely is that, as it evolves, it may need to shift its culture across the quadrant.

Over time, an organization might need to adopt different types of culture, both as the dominant culture, but also specific ones within teams.

Cultural needs can be affected by organizational maturity, size, industry, external competition, and more. An adaptive organization with a clear strategy understands when a different cultural emphasis is needed, whether as the dominant company culture, or as the dominant culture within a specific division, practice area, or team.

For instance, an organization with aggressive growth goals and a reliable product or service may need to shift to a dominant culture of competition in order to meet its objectives. The caution, however, is that if it stays this way for too long, it may lose its focus on innovation at the expense of becoming a sales-driven organization.

A strategic executive team would be able to identify when to modify the cultural focus, and with what teams to make the most drastic changes. In the example above, the sales team within the organization may be the last group within the company to shift even slightly away from a culture of competition, and even then, it may always be the most competition focused. Instead, the product development team may shift to a more collaborative and creative mindset and culture in order to fill the company's pipeline with new and innovative products.

By measuring and understanding a company's culture, leadership is able to adjust factors like the above example in order to maximize revenue potential and long-term growth.

The ideal culture

An organization is an ever-evolving organism, with continually shifting priorities and needs. Its organizational culture is a key component that helps its leadership, employees, partners, and customers understand its focus and values.

The organizational culture assessment framework we've outlined in the preceding pages aims to describe the ideal scenario, where a company understands its desired culture, its current perceived state, and has a plan to reach its ideal state.

This ideal state will have a dominant culture, but never a monolithic one. This is important for many reasons, including the value of diversity (people, ideas, and methods), and the need of an organization to evolve and shift over time (so as not to get "stuck" in one way of being).

A successful culture values alignment, adaptivity, innovation, and diversity in its goals and the strategies used to reach them. The ways in which those goals are achieved may be as diverse as the individuals that make up the organization, but they can all facilitate, measure, and optimize.

Idea starters

A great way to get started with organizational culture is to do an assessment to understand your own organization's culture gap. In my consulting work, I often use my own proprietary culture assessment, but whether you use that one or something similar, it is important to understand both the perceived and desired culture, as well as where leadership needs the culture to shift.

Even more immediately than that, your leadership team can identify their ideal culture and take steps to shift behaviors and incentives to achieve the desired results.

1.5
Component 3: Internal & External Audiences

The ultimate success of the Center of Experience is based on how it is planned, designed, and implemented. This takes a combination of people, processes, and technology in order to achieve. The teams that are involved must be cross-disciplinary, with a full understanding of the holistic experience needs of the enterprise.

This often includes a combination of internal and external teams from a diverse set of backgrounds and expertise including (but not limited to):

- Human resources
- Marketing and Communications
- Customer Experience
- Customer Service

- Operations
- Technology
- Data & Data Science

At this point (and especially since the first edition of this book was written in 2020) many enterprises already have an experience team or department that focuses on at least customer or employee experience, and in some cases both. This team inevitably needs to closely coordinate with the other teams mentioned above to be truly successful in their initiatives, as experience crosses many divisions within any organization.

The Center of Experience recommends a cross-disciplinary team be created and convened on a regular basis, and that its members have close communication, knowledge, and understanding of their respective areas of expertise. Then, this team becomes the central convening body that is ultimately responsible for the success of the Center.

In most cases, this internal team will be augmented by outside firms and individuals with specialization in specific areas. In some cases, an external team will work as facilitators and conveners of the team, which may or may not consist of additional external parties as well.

Working in Agile sprints, this combined team identifies priorities, and works through an iterative process to define requirements and success, design solutions, implement the solutions, and measure the results.

Idea Starter

Ask yourself a question: do you have the right people on your internal teams to accomplish what you need to set up a Center of Experience for your own organization? If you do, that's great. If you're like many others, you may not, and that's where external teams can play a key role. Assess where you think the gaps on your internal team may be and see where external consultants or teams may be able to help.

1.6

Component 4: The 6 Properties

We now come to the inner workings of the Center of Experience. For it to be successful, it requires six different components to all be functioning both independently and in coordination with one another. This incorporates both customer and employee experience together as well.

Figure 1.11 The Center of Experience

The following properties form a complete Center of Experience within an organization. We will review each in much greater detail in Part 2 of this book, but for now let's get a brief overview:

Brand

Measures how advanced an organization is in their adoption of experience-led practices and how well-known they are for those practices.

Governance

This includes the processes and people within an organization that plan, manage, and improve experience programs and initiatives with a company.

Data

These are the components that include customer, employee, and business data, as well as artificial intelligence and other data science-related capabilities.

Environment

This measures the physical and virtual spaces that an organization provides for both employees and customers.

Measurement

These are the methods by which experience itself is measured, and includes the KPIs that drive evolution and change to both customer and employee experience.

Platform

This measures the key foundations an organization needs to be experience-led, from process to the technology infrastructure that powers everything.

There is a lot to explore under each of these topics, which we will do in the chapters that follow.

One potentially obvious yet important thing to note is that each of these properties consists of several different types of people, processes, and technology that are generally not found within a single department. For instance, if the properties were instead things like Marketing, Technology, Human Resources, or other areas that are typically given departments, the Center of Experience might not be necessary. It is for the very reason that experience requires diverse thinking and disciplines that it makes so much sense to approach it in this manner.

We will now review each of the six properties of the Center of Experience in depth in Section Two of this book.

Idea Starter

I've worked with a wide variety of organizations on experience design projects, and while each one is different to some degree, there are a few characteristics that they share. One of these is the fact that there is no one single department, division, or group that owns all aspects of brand experience.

To get started with the properties of the Center of Experience, it would help to understand, within your company, which teams either are responsible for or have a hand in each of the properties we discussed in this chapter. This will help you more easily assemble the teams necessary to be successful.

Part 2:
Properties of the Center of Experience

In this second part of the book, I am going to discuss the individual components of the Center of Experience, which includes their definitions, as well as the processes involved in implementing them.

The goal of this section of the book is to give a practical guide to the six properties which form the central core of the Center of Experience:

2.1
Property 1: Brand

The Center of Experience starts with brand for a few reasons. One, it's the first thing that most audiences will see and experience about an organization, and because of this it has a powerful effect.

While brands have become much more sophisticated over time, there is still a very basic element of recognition and response that benefits successful brands and has very negative effects on brands that make missteps.

While there have been countless definitions of branding over the years, our Center of Experience divides a brand into three primary aspects with two elements that comprise each:

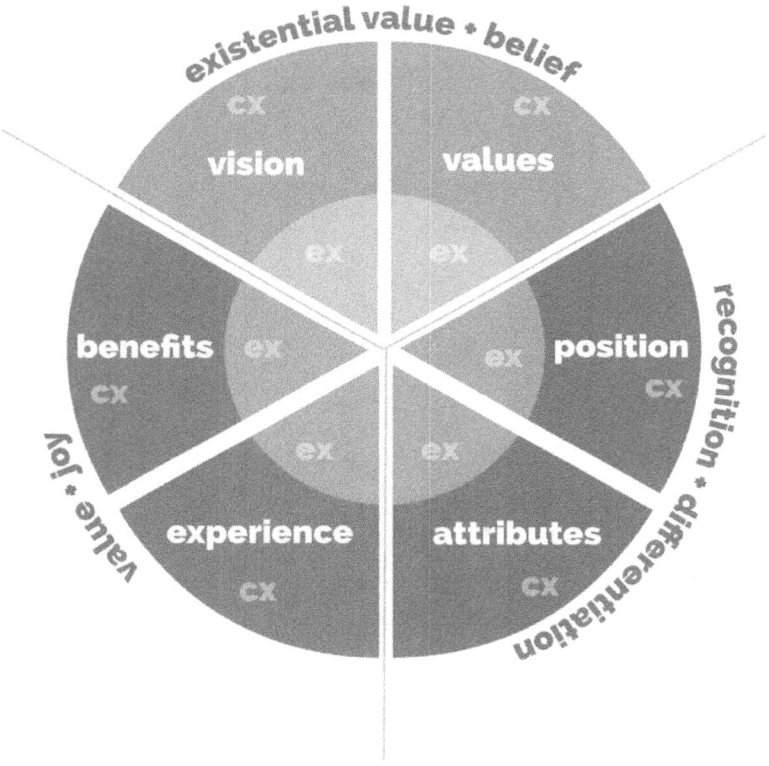

Figure 2.0: The Elements of Brand

The Six Elements of a Brand

As we see in the diagram above, the brand experience framework divides brand into three major categories with two elements in each. Furthermore, each of these elements has both an employee experience and a customer experience component within it, since a brand is both an internal and external expression of an organization. Let's discuss each of the elements of brand in more depth below.

Existential value + belief

We start with how an organization defines its goals and its reason for existence. This category of brand elements is often far-reaching and sometimes abstract, but without practical tools for defining and measuring, it will fail to be successful. Great brands understand this balance.

Vision

This includes a brand's mission, or what it aims to achieve to benefit its customers, employees, shareholders, and the world at large. It also includes its promise to those audiences.

Values

These include what a brand stands for. What will it always (or never) do, and how will it always stay true to its mission? As with all of the other elements of a brand, these values are for both internal and external audiences, though they may be expressed differently for each audience.

Recognition + differentiation

The second group of brand elements relates to how an organization positions itself as relevant to its audiences, and the methods it uses to connect tangibly with its customers, employees, and others.

Position

This defines how an organization distinguishes itself from competitors, and the place a brand occupies in the minds of its audiences. It includes how a brand positions itself both internally and externally.

Attributes

These are the words, symbols and personality a brand chooses to represent itself. While a brand may have variations used for internal and external audiences, the attributes should be cohesive and consistent across all mediums and targets.

Value + joy

The final category of brand elements talks about the emotional aspects of a brand as well as the articulation of the tangible returns its audiences can expect from their experiences.

Experience

This is how audiences interact, communicate, and consume a brand's products and services. It includes both the customer and employee experience.

Benefits

This defines the value proposition that audiences get from their interactions with the brand and its products and services, as well as the tangible value gained. While this varies greatly depending on the brand (e.g. quick service restaurant versus investment firm), it is a critical aspect of a brand, nonetheless.

Brand audiences

Internal

As its label would suggest, these audiences are those that are within a company or organization. Employees, board members, shareholders, and others with knowledge and input on the inner workings of the company comprise this group.

Often, a company will have a unique way of presenting itself to these groups, though to be successful it must align with the external brand.

External

This group consists of current and prospective customers, and other groups that don't have direct lines of communication or input on the brand itself. While successful brands find ways to gather feedback and communication from external audiences, they are always shown a specific "view" of the brand that is often different in nature than the internal one.

Other

This final category could almost be construed as another internal or external set of audiences, depending on how you look at it. Think about partner channels, vendors, and other individuals and companies that interact with your organization regularly.

This "other" category can be very important because of its network effect. For instance, a partner or vendor that has a lot of mutual or potential customers could either greatly help or hurt a brand's reputation depending on the motivation.

Distinguishing between "branding" and "brand experience"

Branding, as defined within the context of the Center of Experience, is a key aspect and, because of its highly visible nature, is the property we address first. First and foremost, however, we want to concern ourselves with brand *experience* when discussing COX.

When we refer to branding, we refer to the subjective and objective ways that one company or product sets itself apart from its competition, as defined above in the discussion on the six elements. While branding is a wide-ranging discipline with many aspects this book cannot possibly cover in depth, the subject of brand experience is both different in aim and broader in scope.

Brand experience, on the other hand, is the sum of all the interactions, interfaces, and any other touchpoints that all audiences have with a company or product. The role of the Center of Experience is to ensure that the brand experience is optimal for all audiences.

While branding is often a collection of items dictated by a brand for customers to consume, brand *experience* is often a two-way dialog between the two.

Successful brands

A brand that is deemed successful has alignment across its audiences on all of its individual elements, and there is a long-term plan to maintain this alignment. While individual elements may evolve over time, a brand's identifiability, cohesion, and demonstration of value to its audiences ultimately determines its long-term success.

Idea starter

You may not sit on the corporate branding team, but it doesn't mean you shouldn't thoroughly understand your company's vision, mission and values. Your team should also understand and exemplify these.

As an exercise, review the last one or two large initiatives your team completed and ask yourself if your team's execution and attitude while completing these initiatives demonstrated the values of your organization, and accomplished something in line with its mission. If you can answer "yes," or even "mostly," that is good news.

If not, why is that the case? Is it because the brand has not been communicated clearly enough or is it not something that is made central to the work your team performs?

2.2
Property 2: Governance

In the Center of Experience, governance defines how both customer and employee experience follow internally as well as externally established guidelines and regulations.

These are the methods that are used to ensure customer and employee experience are performing consistently, ethically, and according to applicable internal and external guidelines and regulations.

These processes include the following two primary groupings, and four underlying criteria for evaluating success in Governance of customer and employee experience:

Figure 2.1: The Center of Experience Governance Elements

Each of these elements includes a set of guidelines, processes, and often documentation that assists in their application and enforcement. While we won't be sharing all of those items in this book, we'll touch on what should be included in each. Let's explore these in more detail in the pages that follow.

Group 1: Definition and Collaboration

The first group consists of the areas where we are establishing how governance is communicated, as well as how the teams involved are structured and involved.

Area 1: Clarity

Are the policies/regulations clearly defined and are the processes required explained well? Do the teams both tasked with following the policies/regulations, as well as enforcing them, understand what is expected of them?

Experience Vision and Manifesto

Regardless of common underlying processes and methodologies, every organization approaches customer experience and employee experience in a unique way. Creating an Experience Manifesto helps an organization align around a common purpose and definition of what great experience means to its specific customers, employees, and partners.

Business objectives

While the manifesto spells out the vision in words that everyone involved can easily remember and internalize in their daily tasks, it is also critical to define the key business objectives as they relate to experience. This will ultimately result in metrics or key performance indicators (KPIs) being defined. The **Governance** component within the Center of Experience model is related to the **Measurement** component by these business objectives.

Policy definition

After the vision for experience is laid out for the organization, a clear set of policies, processes, roles, and responsibilities must be defined. Because experience is something that every employee takes part in, and is affected by, these guidelines need to account for everyone's unique role. In the Coordination section, we'll talk more about what those roles and responsibilities should be.

Internal Communications

Finally, after defining the vision, tying business objectives to the vision, and articulating policy and processes, it is time to communicate this to the teams involved. Internal communications can (and should) take many forms, from educational meetings or sessions, webinars, documentation, and other methods.

It is worth underscoring just how important the internal communications piece of this is. Even the best process or policy is only as good as how well it is understood and implemented by the teams tasked with doing so.

Area 2: Coordination

Do teams understand their roles, and are they empowered to be successful? What roles are needed and what relationship do they have with each other and the tasks to be performed?

The governance process requires coordination among departments, teams, and roles within teams. While every organization is structured differently, there are distinct roles in relation to the experience governance process that generally do not change.

Governance process

The following five roles comprise those needed to perform governance of experience within an organization. These roles will likely be spread across an organization and there might be several that are sitting within distinct teams.

The roles are as follows:

- **Oversight**

  This role holds the critical component of ensuring that the Center of Experience is operating smoothly, and that the people, processes, and technology continue to remain integrated and running smoothly.

- **Review**

  This role is responsible for reading and understanding processes and requirements and ensuring they are accurately documented and that there are understandable procedures in place to implement them.

- **Auditing**

  This role tests and verifies that the review team has created processes that are easily understood, enforceable, and measurable. In the software development world, they would be the quality assurance team that tests and verifies that everything is usable and repeatable.

- **Revisions**

  The process of reviewing and revising processes and the tasks and documents associated with them is critical. Thus, these three roles are very important and related.

- **Improvement**

  Although a chief component of governance is in maintaining a consistent approach, there must always be a desire for continuous improvement. Thus, improvement must be a process with roles assigned in order to always be looking for ways to make the system better.

Process and Enforcement

The second group relates to how governance is performed, evaluated, and administered within an organization.

Area 3: Consistency

Are the teams regularly complying with stated policies/regulations? Are policies/regulations evenly applied to applicable teams and functions across the organization?

Guidelines and Measurement

While the exact guidelines and measurements will vary based on the organization, these are critical to the success of any experience initiative.

Enforcement

As we saw earlier in the governance process under "Coordination," the following areas also need to be enforced:

- Oversight
- Review
- Auditing
- Revisions
- Improvement

Ensuring that all the functions in these areas are being performed and are following agreed-upon processes and policies is critical.

Area 4: Compliance

This includes how both customer and employee experience adhere to internal and external policies and regulations, and the process by which compliance is reviewed. This also includes how non-compliance or adherence to processes and regulations is addressed or enforced.

A comprehensive investment in experience requires ensuring legal and ethical compliance across a broad range of issues.

External Compliance

For customer experience, this includes addressing privacy concerns, such as those regulated by GDPR, or accessibility needs, as regulated by the U.S. Rehabilitation Act of 1975 (commonly referred to as "Section 508"), or the Americans with Disabilities Act (ADA), including many other areas.

For employee experience this ranges from HIPAA compliance, to other privacy requirements needed when dealing with personally identifiable information (PII), and many other laws and guidelines.

Internal Compliance

There are also internal policies, values, and ethics that an organization will need to enforce. This includes ensuring internal team members are following the guidelines articulated in the Clarity section of this document, as well as following the processes and guidelines formalized and agreed to..

It can also apply to all of the other aspects that comprise the Center of Experience, such as communication policies, data science and artificial intelligence policies, privacy guidelines, and many others.

Accountability

Last, but certainly not least, it should go without saying that accountability is a large part of governance, but a global component of compliance is the accountability within an organization to remain compliant and adhering to all internal and external processes, rules and regulations. In many cases, the stakes are high, as non-compliance can incur fines or worse.

Thus, accountability is a critical component and must be part of both the processes as well as the culture of the organization.

Process and its application can have a huge effect on employees and customers. With employees, for instance, according to Gallup, 88% of employees think their employer did a poor job with the onboarding process,[27] and 32% of global executives rate the onboarding they receive as poor according to Harvard Business Review[28]. Is this a matter of a process not being in place, not being followed, or not being followed consistently? Good governance can help with these issues.

Governance is an enterprise-wide effort, and thus the teams involved will undoubtedly comprise a cross-section of members from many disciplines. Having these teams read from the same playbook makes the Center of Experience run smoothly and effectively.

Idea Starter

To have true governance for your Center of Experience, you need to have a good handle on the processes and teams that are currently responsible for them. A good way to start would be to do your own audit of the processes that you have in place to ensure good customer and employee experiences.

2.3

COX Property 3: Data

We won't be spending quite as much time or space on this item as some of the others, as I covered this quite extensively in both of my books, *House of the Customer* (2023) as well as *Meaningful Measurement of the Customer Experience* (2022), I want to make sure at least cover a few of the key points, and make sure to underscore that data is a very important components of our Center of Experience.

Let's look at a few aspects of data that are most directly relevant to our Center of Experience.

Experience and Operational Data

In my book, *Meaningful Measurement of the Customer Experience* (2022), I explore several categories of data, but I'm going to keep things a little simpler here, though I encourage you to read that book as well when you are tasked with the measurement components of your work. That said, when discussing customer experience, there are often two primary types discussed: operational data and experience data. It's essential to understand the difference between the two to use them effectively.

Operational Data

Operational data refers to the data that pertains to the functioning and performance of a product or service. This type of data is collected automatically by an organization's systems, and it helps in analyzing performance levels, identifying errors, and overall operation of the organization.

This data is usually structured, collected in a centralized database and is decision-oriented. Examples of operational data include sales data, inventory levels, website traffic, and customer churn rates. This type of data is useful in identifying areas that need improvement and also in studying past trends to improve future performances.

Experience Data

Unlike operational data, experience data is subjective and usually based on customer interaction and feedback. It refers to the data collected from customer feedback, reviews, surveys, behavioral data, and social media interactions.

Experience data helps marketers to gain insights into how customers feel, their thoughts, and opinions about a brand, product, or service. Experience data is primarily collected through qualitative research and is unstructured, context-dependent, and subjective.

Examples of experience data include reviews, social media comments, and customer service feedback.

Why Both are Important

Both operational and experience data are crucial to enhance customer experience and boost the bottom line of any business. Operational data helps businesses understand how the company is performing, identify bottlenecks, and streamline operations to optimize performance. On the other hand, experience data enables businesses to gain insights into customer sentiment, understanding what drives customer loyalty, and areas for improvement. By combining both operational and experience data, marketers can tailor their campaigns to the needs of their customers, improving their experience.

How to Leverage Both

One effective way to leverage operational and experience data is to integrate them into a centralized system. For instance, by integrating data from customer service queries with operational data such as sales data, businesses can identify correlations between a particular product or feature and customer dissatisfaction.

This means that leveraging both types of data is essential in building a strategy that leads to customer satisfaction, enhanced customer experience, and ultimately increased revenue.

Data science and AI

There is no way to do a subject like artificial intelligence justice in the space of a few paragraphs, but I will keep it brief, nonetheless. Any data plans need to involve incorporation of AI, and here are a few areas to explore:

- Consideration of several types of AI tools, including generative AI, predictive analytics, and workflow automation
- Governance of AI, including how models are reviewed, and how transparent your processes and tools are that utilize AI
- Ethics of AI, including protecting against bias

There is certainly more to explore in this area, and it is probably the most fast-moving of any of the areas touched on in this book. I spend much more time on this topic in my other book, The Agile Brand Guide to AI & Marketing, including a deeper review of the types of AI tools, and more.

Citizen data scientists

The last brief point I'll cover here relates to just how accessible AI-based tools have become so recently. As of writing this revised edition in the Summer of 2023, all things artificial intelligence seem to have descended on the world of work and it doesn't seem to be showing any signs of stopping.

One of the many interesting phenomena is the idea of the citizen data scientist, or the non-technical person who is able to manipulate and use data without a team of data scientists behind them writing SQL scripts, or scripts in Python, R, or other programming languages.

Instead, the citizen data scientist is able to do a lot with low-code or no-code tools, using a "drag and drop" interface to perform complex calculations and tasks. As you plan your Center of Experience, I highly recommend you consider building out your data components in a way that incorporates the citizen data scientist as a key part of the team. Note that this isn't a *replacement* for trained and skilled data scientist, but rather an *augmentation*.

Conclusion

Data is a crucial part of the customer experience and marketing world, and understanding the difference between operational and experience data is essential to unlocking actionable insights. By combining both data types, businesses can tailor campaigns towards their customers uniquely, leading to improved customer experience, increased brand loyalty, and ultimately greater revenue.

Then, by layering in intentional and judicious use of artificial intelligence tools based on the work of your data science teams and models, you can best be set up to anticipate the world of what's to come, including setting up your own Center of Experience.

2.4
Property 4: Environment

Sometimes when we think of work environment, we might only consider the immediate workspaces of employees. Patagonia understands its employees' greater needs as well. They provide on-site childcare, which while expensive to the company, helps them retain great employees, including the 70 percent of woman in upper management.

They also famously allow employees to set their work schedule to allow them to surf at the best times. "We have a policy that when the surf comes up, you drop work and you go surfing," says Yvon Chouinard, founder and owner of Patagonia[29].

In addition to the physical and virtual ones, this is clearly an overall work environment based on understanding that hiring the right employees and trusting them to do the right thing goes a long way toward the success of the company.

Despite some examples like Patagonia, the vast majority of employees believe their current workplace environment is lacking. According to a recent study by Fellowes, over three quarters of those workers surveyed would like their current employer to offer healthier workspace benefits, with things like wellness rooms, company fitness benefits, sit-stands, healthy lunch options and ergonomic seating[30].

In the Center of Experience, environment consists of the "places" aspect of experience. This includes both physical and virtual spaces where employees interact, as well as where customers interact with a brand (Figure 2.9).

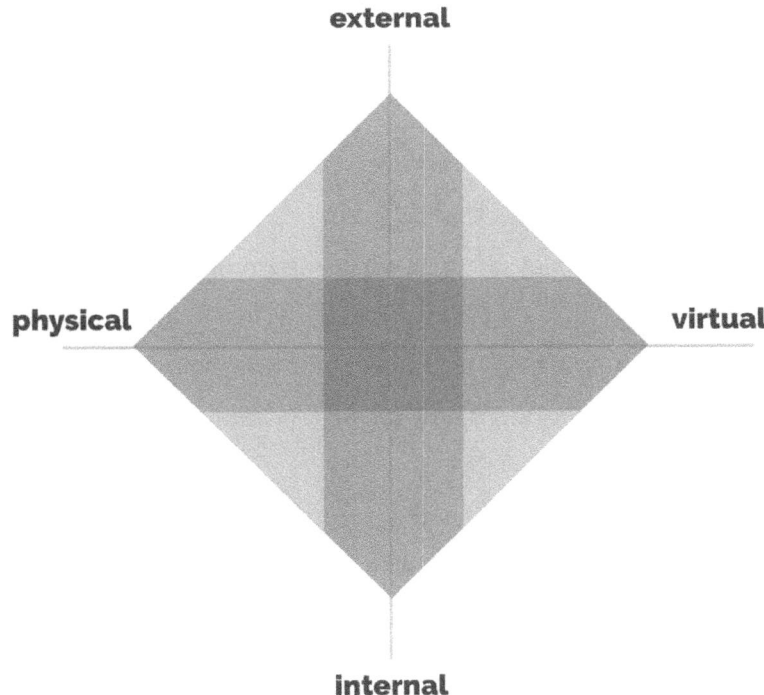

Figure 2.9: Environment in the Center of Experience

Audiences

Let's start by talking about the two categories of audiences: employees and customers.

Employee

It is highly likely that a company's employees are the ones who spend the most time in both physical and virtual environments. This includes:

- Physical work environment such as office, conference rooms and desks/cubicles
- Virtual environments such as online workspaces, conferencing technologies

Because of the nature of their usage, environment requires different design considerations than customer-facing environments. For instance, because employees in an office environment often work eight-hour plus days from a single location, their design and experience considerations must be different than a customer-facing location where a customer might only spend a few hours a year at most.

Don't rule out seemingly small improvements, either. In the workplace, an improvement of increased fresh air was shown to increase productivity by 11% in research carried out by the World

Green Building Council[31]. That's quite a result from something as simple as windows that open!

Customer

A central tenet of the Center of Experience approach is that intrinsically motivated employees are the "engine" that truly power great experiences. This is evident in the environment category and manifests in important ways.

From a customer perspective, this includes:

- Physical environments such as retail stores or service centers
- Virtual environments such as websites, social media, or customer service lines

Partner

There is another category that is external to the organization, and this includes partners and vendors. We treat them as an "external" audiences, though most often these groups have a level of access to both physical and virtual environments that exceeds that of the other external audience, customers.

While it probably goes without saying, the partner experience within physical and virtual environments can make a critical difference to key relationships within an organization. This varies from making it easier for resellers to generate more sales revenue to maintaining a stellar reputation with critical suppliers.

Overlaps

Also note in the Figure 2.9 above that there are "overlapping" areas. Because customer experience and employee experience have many interdependencies, many of both the physical and virtual environments are shared between both groups.

Environment leaves a lasting first impression and has been shown to influence employee productivity and retention. Despite this, a recent Gensler survey showed that only 25% of U.S.-based office employees considered themselves to have optimal work environments[32].

Types of environments

Moving on from our discussion of audiences, we will now start talking about the types of environments that comprise both customer and employee experiences.

Physical Environments

Let's start our discussion of the types of environments with the physical ones.

According to a 2014 study by TemaNord of companies across Scandinavia in several industries, they were able to find a strong correlation between employee productivity and the quality of physical environment[33]. In fact, physical environment was deemed to have a greater impact on productivity and quality of work than other psychosocial or wellbeing factors.

While we already gave some examples of physical environments in the audiences section, we can just briefly recap by saying that these are the places where employees go (such as an office), or where customers interact with a brand that are owned by the organization, such as a brick and mortar store for a retailer, a classroom building for a university, or an office building for an employee.

Note that we qualify these environments by saying they are "owned" by the company, so things like a customer's house, or a customer's office don't fall in this category. Instead, those two examples would more likely fall in the next, virtual, category, since those audiences are interacting with the company's products and services remotely (virtually) from those physical environments.

Virtual Environments

Moving on to digital and virtual environments, the following are just a few examples of what can be included in this category:

- External
    - Marketing Website
    - Customer Portals and Other Communication Tools (chatbots, etc.)
    - Social Media
    - Virtual Reality Product Demos
- Internal
    - Intranets
    - Virtual Meeting Spaces or Conference Lines

It is important to note that for internal environments, there is a distinction between environment and application, which is covered in the COX platform property. So, things like Human Resources Information Systems (HRIS) or the apps that an employee uses day to day are covered under platform instead.

Environment, or the places both physical and virtual that your audiences experience your brand, is a critical component of the Center of Experience. The quality of environment can transform a good experience into a great one and is just as likely to leave a poor lasting impression if it doesn't live up to expectations.

Similar to the other properties of the Center of Experience, though, it is an interdependent component. This means that it relies heavily on everything from the platforms that run the virtual environments, to the brand messaging, and the look and feel that inform the design of a product or a retail store.

Idea Starters

One idea that includes an overlap between physical and virtual environments is the following: Consider personalizing the employee experience within a physical environment by using digital identify to control access to buildings and other areas. Isn't it time you stopped using access cards and let your employees use their smartphone (which is with them all the time anyway) to access everything?

Now, take this a step further. When you know a *customer* is in one of your physical environments, what could you do to enhance the experience? Many retailers are already utilizing tracking and other tools, but there are a lot of opportunities to find creative solutions to do more than observe.

2.5
Property 5: Measurement

In the CMO Survey[34] I mentioned earlier, it is also interesting to note that the second top challenge faced in managing customer experience is determining the contribution of each touchpoint to the overall customer experience and identifying all critical touchpoints. There are several other challenges in a list of 10 that also relate to measurement in some way or another.

Measuring Success with the Center of Experience

Measurement is broken down into five primary categories:

- **Quantitative**
  Things that can be objectively measured
- **Qualitative**
  Things that can be subjectively measured
- **Process**
  The workflows and systems that enable customer experience and employee experience to occur

- **Product**

  The tools and services the organization produces for both external and internal audiences

- **Global**

  Composite scores or other metrics that span multiple categories

Note that you can use these metrics for both customer experience as well as employee experience, though the sources may vary drastically. These combined measurement elements give a holistic picture of an organization's performance related to experience investments and programs.

Success with the Center of Experience

While achieving success is covered within the measurement property of the Center of Experience, ultimate success will be measured on sustained performance over time. This means that consistent, and consistently growing numbers are achieved in the long term. It also means that success should be mapped from the starting point of the Center of Experience, or employee motivation, all the way through to tangible returns. This is one of the most powerful aspects of this framework.

Thus, the Center of Experience allows an organization to start at the individual employee level and ultimately achieve real, tangible results, or plainly put, dollars and cents that are directly attributable to an investment in employee and customer experience. A demonstration of how this achieved is in the figure below (Figure 2.11):

Inputs

Individual	Organizational	External
EX	**EX**	**CX**
Employee motivation	Organizational culture health	Customer Experience Metrics
	Employee Experience Metrics	

Influences

EX	CX
Employee Retention	Customer Acquisition
Employee Productivity	Customer Retention
	Deal Size

Outcomes

Savings	Revenue
Cost savings due to higher employee retention	Increased revenue due to increased employee productivity
	Increased revenue due to increased customer sales and retention

Figure 2.11: How success is measured with the Center of Experience

You can see how everything starts with the individual employee, and intrinsic motivators, and flows out to the organization, then customers, and ultimately produces both savings in terms of increased retention, as well as revenue in terms of increased employee productivity and customer sales and retention.

This is how the Center of Experience provides a holistic combination of people, processes, and technology that transforms organizations and produces return on experience.

System of continuous improvement

A robust measurement system would not be complete without a method to ensure its continued success.

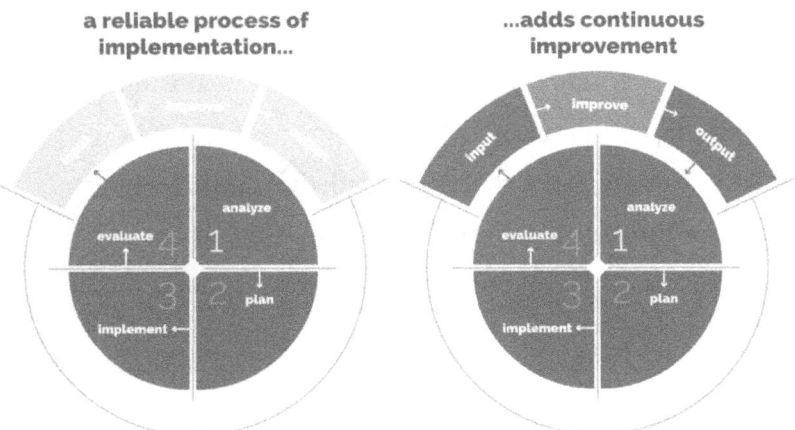

Figure 2.12: Continuous improvement in the measurement property

Thus, a system of continuous improvement is built into the Center of Experience. This takes a series of steps that include the following:

1. Analyze
2. Plan
3. Implement
4. Evaluate

And adds three important ones:

1. **Input**

   Take the evaluation criteria and let them form the basis for the improvement

2. **Improve**

   Define the methods and processes by which improvements will be delivered

3. **Output**

   Deliver those improvements to the teams responsible for continuing the process

As you can see in the chart provided, the last three steps provide this continuous improvement method. This process will require people, processes and technology in order to successfully achieve.

The return on employee experience

While I could discuss the same about the customer experience, let's briefly discuss what the return on investment on EX can look like in the real world. You will also see how closely EX and CX are related as well.

Employee experience an increasing priority among companies of all sizes for obvious reasons. With a competitive job market, continual disruption in established industries, and a growing shift in salaried workers into the gig economy, finding ways to keep employees engaged and happy in their positions is a commonsense approach to reduce turnover and motivate employees to do their best work.

While this sounds like common sense, most organizations need more practical justifications to invest in enhancing EX. This means finding the return on investment (ROI) in employee experience initiatives. My agency works with companies of all sizes to find the best and most meaningful methods to do this. We will discuss several of these below.

Tangible benefits of great employee experience

The best way to show return on investment on EX is to use metrics that are easily measured. Here are some of the more concrete and measurable returns on great employee experience.

Let's start with increased employee retention. According to TLNT, replacing an employee can cost an organization anywhere from 30% of an entry level salary to 400% of a senior executive's salary[35]. That's a compelling reason to invest in improved employee experience.

Greater productivity is more easily measured in some organizations versus others, but it is important to every organization.

According to Gallup, there is a confirmed connection between engaged employees and an increase in productivity[36]. Engaged employees are most often those who experience a superior EX.

Increased customer satisfaction is another measurable outcome of great employee experience. Customer experience has gotten a lot of attention from organizations, where marketing departments are starting to understand how critical experience is to customer acquisition and retention. But what, you ask, does customer satisfaction have to do with employee experience? What you get on the inside you get on the outside. In other words, happy employees help create happy customers. You can see this in the example of Chick-fil-A, where an emphasis on employee experience has created a fast food chain that earns nearly double the per-store sales of its next closest competitor, McDonald's[37].

Less tangible benefits of great employee experience

The section above showed several examples that my agency has used to demonstrate how an investment in employee experience can directly pay off. Now let's explore a few slightly less concrete benefits that, while more difficult to measure, are still inextricably linked to a highly engaged workforce.

Greater innovation is hard to quantify, but invaluable to any organization. In the section above where we discussed tangible benefits, we mentioned increased productivity as an outcome of improved employee engagement. Another byproduct of engagement that stems from improved employee experience is the creation of better products and services, and better solutions to both internal and external challenges. More engaged employees can be much more empathetic to coworkers and to the customers they service. This allows them to come up with more relevant and often better ideas that help a company stay innovative and ahead of the competition.

Easier recruiting is often a reason that companies invest in talent branding initiatives. It is true that any branding effort, internal or external, can often pique interests and capture the imaginations of prospective candidates (or customers). But, as sites such as Comparably or Glassdoor have proven, a great-sounding tagline for your talent brand can fall flat if the actual experience of your employees isn't truly great. Instead, investments in great employee experience with a talent brand to match are a winning combination that provides a more seamless recruiting process and can expand your candidate pool to better candidates.

As you can see, there are many different ways that investments in improved employee experience can pay off. Whether they are more tangible, such as decreased turnover rates, or less directly measurable, such as an increase in innovation, focusing on improving EX is worth the effort.

Idea Starters

A good way to get started with measurement is to understand what the ultimate KPIs are. That will let you work backwards from them and design both experiences, as well as the measurements of those experiences, that are aligned with core business objectives.

You could even start with KPIs or key measurements in your respective area of the organization. How does experience relate to how your success is measured? Answering that question will provide a great starting point.

2.6
Property 6: Platform

The tools, processes and methods used to create experiences are critical to tasks being performed well, to engaging and retaining both customers and employees, as well as creating a sustainable set of business practices based around experience.

Too often the platform component of experience is overlooked or assumptions are made that elements simply can't be changed or might be too complex to change. Some of this is a problem in itself, which has caused organizations to invest in creating component architecture from their formerly monolithic systems.

This component-based mindset allows an organization to be more agile and make changes as needed across the enterprise.

Despite this, challenges still exist. On the employee side, a recent PwC Tech at Work study of 12,000 international employees found that while 90% of C-Suite executives said their company pays attention to their employee's needs when introducing new technology, only 53% of their staff said the same thing.

Clearly there is room to grow in the platform element of experience.

While we list platform last in the properties of the Center of Experience, it is by no means the least important. In fact, one could say that without the right platforms, great experiences would not be possible.

There are six primary components of Platform that we break into three categories (Figure 2.13):

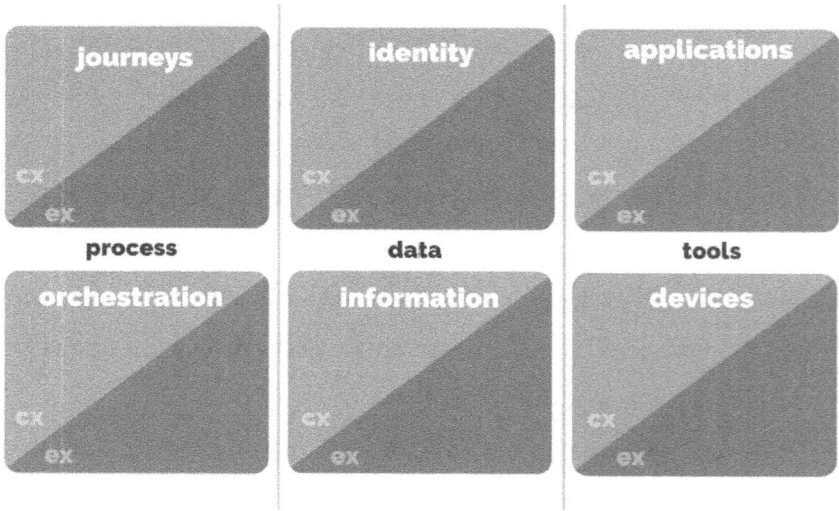

Figure 2.13: Platform and the Center of Experience

Category 1: Process

The first category of platforms within the Center of Experience relates to the systems of interaction. This is how experiences are defined and played out for both customers and employees.

Journeys

The first component of Platform we'll discuss is the journey. To optimize and experience, we must understand what the ideal sequence of events should be. As you can see in the diagrams below, the customer experience and employee experience differ greatly, but both have consistent journeys that can be designed and optimized for better experience.

Customer Experience

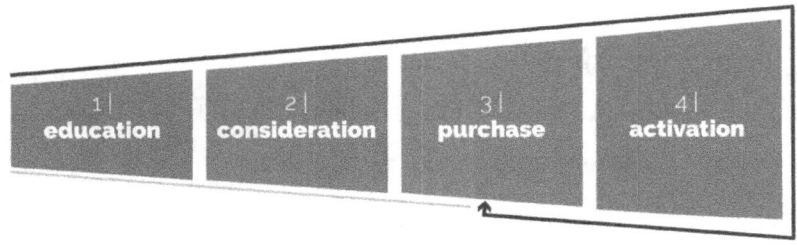

Figure 2.14: The customer journey

The stages in the customer experience are the following:

- **Education**

  The buyer is aware they have a challenge but are unaware of the proper solution. During this stage they might even discover the true definition and nature of their challenge.

- **Consideration**

  The buyer understands their challenge well enough to begin comparing potential solutions and narrows their competitive set.

- **Purchase**

  The buyer chooses a product or service and makes the purchase.

- **Activation**

  The buyer begins using the product or service and has the potential to become an advocate and/or repeat buyer.

Employee Experience

Unlike the customer experience, the employee experience (Figure 2.15) has a few stages within it which are not ones that we necessarily want the person to accelerate through too quickly.

This illustrates some of the fundamental differences between customer and employee experience, in that with the latter, the desired result is not a speedy and decisive movement through to the end of the process. This is because, of course, the last step in the employee experience is an employee transitioning out of the company. In most cases, this is not the desired result.

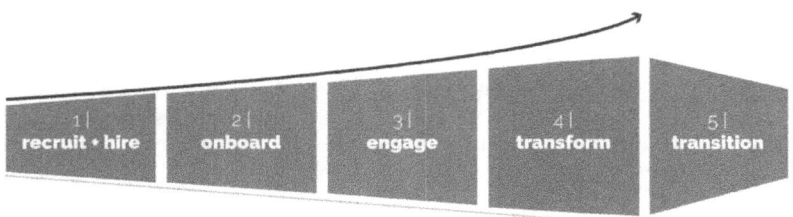

Figure 2.15: The employee journey

The stages in the employee experience consist of the following:

- **Recruit + hire**

  The employee and employer are assessing the best fit based on needs and requirements

- **Onboard**

  The employee becomes acclimated to the new systems and process of the organization

- **Engage**

  The employee becomes productive and an active member of the organization

- **Transform**

  The employee seeks growth and is presented with opportunities to advance their position and professional expertise, as well as their contributions to the company

- **Transition**

  The employee begins their search for a different opportunity and leaves the organization, is terminated, or retires

Your organization may have several other types of journeys and experiences that require a journey map. For instance, a university would have a student journey. A trade or membership association would have a membership journey. A technology company might have a partner or vendor journey.

As you can see, all of these journeys require a combination of people, processes, and technology in order to accomplish. Thus, this reinforces that "platform" is a combination of all three of those things.

Orchestration

This describes how identities, devices, and applications work together in order to provide an exceptional experience. This relates closely to the Journey portion of the platform pillar but is defined separately here because orchestration is as much about how systems and processes relate to one another (its close relation to journeys) as the technical and data integration between them.

Orchestration can provide many benefits, from reducing human error to providing a more personalized experience to audiences. In more sophisticated organizations, tools like customer journey orchestration (CJO) tools are used to achieve this.

Category 2: Data

The second category of platforms includes all of the data needed in order to provide great experiences to employees and customers.

Identity

This includes how digital identities are managed for both customers and employees, as well as how data is stored that relates to the customer or employee experience.

Note that this is a wide-ranging component that touches on many other components identified within other pillars, including journeys (identity and person-specific information is valuable throughout), compliance (personally identifiable information is subject to a good deal of regulation), and many others.

Identity includes an internal (employees) and external (customers and partners) component, and how each are treated can greatly affect the return on experience.

For instance, for both internal and external audiences, personally relevant information and interactions is key. So much so, that 80% of consumers say that they are more likely to make a purchase if they are offered a personalized experience[38]. The important thing to note, of course, is that employees are also consumers and are used to this type of treatment outside of the office. Employers who understand this and embrace personalizing the work experience have a lot to gain as well.

Information

This includes the storage of information that is not necessarily person-specific, but still relevant to experience, such as process documentation, source code for applications, and many other possibilities.

Information can be categorized as internal, external, or shared. This creates a need for taxonomies and classification of information, as well as a close tie to identity and devices, for both security and personalization.

Category 3: Tools

The last category under Platform involves the software and hardware that customers, employees and other audiences use in order to connect with a brand, and in order to solve challenges or complete tasks.

Applications

These are the individual programs that an employee or customer might interact with in order to complete an individual task, or part of their journey.

For customers and other external audiences, these are often exclusively either web-based or mobile apps, since most of the applications a customer uses to interact with brands are more widely available things like web browsers.

For employees, this could be a combination of many things, including the applications they are given access to based on their role or other permissions. I can also say this has a tangible impact on employees. Sixty percent of workers, for instance, will say that access to the right mobile technology increases their productivity[39].

It also includes the communication channels owned and managed by the organization (e.g. HRIS, intranets, and CRMs for employees; and websites, social media platforms, and SMS for customers.

Devices

This includes the company-owned or managed devices that customers or employees use and interact with.

For employees, this is everything from desktop computers, laptops, tablets and smartphones that they are either provided by their employer or bring to work and use as part of their job. Some 67% of employees use personal devices at work already, and 87% of businesses are dependent on their employees' ability to access their mobile business apps from their personal smartphone, despite not officially allowing them in the workplace[40].

To optimize the employee experience, many companies are implementing a BYOD, or bring-your-own-device policy. As the name suggests, this allows employees to work on their device of choice and with the tools they are most comfortable with. The statistics surrounding this are pretty compelling as well. According to ITProPortal, companies gain an extra 240 hours of work per year from employees due to mobile working[41].

For customers, this might include a kiosk used in a retail environment, or another company-owned device that customers interact with a company on.

While for customer experience, this technically could be any device sold by the organization, when thinking in terms of the Center of Experience, we prefer to confine them to devices *owned* by the company itself. This is what distinguishes the "devices" category from the next category of "applications."

Idea Starter

Does your team have the platforms and tools to be truly successful? What would help them provide better experiences for your key audiences? Many times, an enterprise will invest in systems that offer an extraordinary amount of power, features, and flexibility to employees, yet they don't do a great job of educating them. So, you have an amazing set of tools, but you don't really know what you have. Or, as an IT Director I recently met with from a transportation company told me, "I feel like the company bought me a Ferrari, but won't let me take it out of second gear."

One thing you can do is open up the hood on that Ferrari and see if there are features and functionality available to you and your team that might be able to provide a better experience to your audiences.

Part 3:
Implementation

In this section, we're going to explore the practical application of the tools and methods of the Center of Experience, as well as a few tools that you can use to best implement it within your organization.

These include some practical tips and ideas of how to get started with the ideas discussed earlier, as well as some tools that are helpful in implementing the Center of Experience, such as an experience maturity model, as well as the Next Best Action model that lies at the center of great customer and employee journeys.

3.0
Let's talk about silos

To get started with the section on application of the Center of Experience, we should start with the organization itself and some potential roadblocks you will need to overcome to be successful.

Why is experience challenging?

Many organizations find it so challenging to truly embrace the combination of customer experience and employee experience, or what the Center of Experience refers to as brand experience, because of legacy structures, processes, and even software and data. So, it comes back to people, processes, and technology that are now preventing better experiences and the processes and methods that enable them.

The reasons for this are many, but one slightly obvious one is that no one was thinking about either customer or employee experience (let alone *both together)* when the organizational structures that currently exist in most companies were created.

Marketing communicated to support sales. Sales talked to customers before they bought. Customer service listened to customer feedback and complaints after they purchased. Human resources handled all things related to employees. IT got requests from departments and fulfilled them. All of these things happened in silos, and for the most part it worked okay. Or did it?

Often, as long as numbers were positive, whether that was sales, retention, or otherwise, the loss of efficiency or customer discontent due to all the silos either slipped under radar, or in the case of many smaller organizations, there wasn't sophisticated enough measurement in the first place to truly understand what was happening.

In my book, *The Agile Consumer (2019)*, I discussed the evolution in the relationship between brands and consumers and how the increase in variety, access, and control that customers now have has shifted us into a world where brands compete primarily based on experience and relationship.

This shift, combined with companies' increased ability to analyze and understand their data (thank you, Big Data) has allowed organizations to truly understand the effect that experience can have on the bottom line.

As this realization has been sweeping the business world, there has been another realization that has quickly followed it: *Experience isn't easy to do well.*

Ownership of experience

This is due in part because of a fundamental question: Who owns experience? Chief Experience Officers and experience teams are popping up at more organizations, but as they will surely tell you, a single team can't easily manage the entire customer experience, let alone the brand experience, which includes employees as well.

Instead, experience is a cross-disciplinary effort across a company that might be *led* by one team, but involves brand, marketing, HR, technology, operations, customer service, product, sales, and potentially many others.

What does success look like?

While every organization varies to a degree, there are some approaches that I would suggest starting with. Let's explore these below.

Ad hoc experience group

If there isn't an experience team already at your organization, you would do well to convene a cross-disciplinary group that works across the customer and employee experience. You may choose to start by focusing only on one or the other (customer or employee), but keep in mind that if you start with customers not employees, you are short-changing the process. Motivated employees in a customer-centric culture are at the heart of the Center of Experience for a reason.

This cross-disciplinary group should have a goal and associated timeline in which to achieve that goal. It also needs some senior buy-in so that the ideas generated can more easily get traction.

Pilot experience project

If your organization already has a team dedicated to experience, the next step would be to create a pilot project that ties together both customer and employee experience into a true *brand experience* initiative.

This might be a limited effort, but it needs to be comprehensive to be ultimately beneficial. Find a way to tie things from employee to customer experience, end to end, and put some measurements of success in place.

Center of Experience

If you are even further along as an organization, my suggestion would be to put the pieces in place to start setting up a Center of Experience. I will go into detail about how to do this in the next chapter.

Idea starters

If none of the above ideas are quite the best fit, here's one more.

One idea I highly recommend is (if convening a Center of Excellence or even a company-wide, cross-disciplinary team is too much to start) to start talking and working with one or two team members on a different team within your organization. If you sit on the human resources team, this might mean starting to have deeper conversations with someone from the technology team to see what barriers they run into in implementing more employee-friendly software or hardware solutions. Or if you are in brand marketing, talk with customer service to hear what your product or services customers are *really* saying.

While your company most likely has data and a dashboard associated with some of these questions, you'd be surprised what having some conversations can do to expand your thinking and help you find new solutions to experienced challenges.

3.1
Getting started

Let's now discuss some recommendations of how to implement a Center of Experience within your organization. To do this, we're going to use a familiar framework (with one addition at the end) to do so. We will discuss the people, process, and technology needed to create a Center of Experience, and end with a fourth category: measures of success.

People

As we see at the very center of the Center of Experience, motivated employees are at the heart of success. Those happy employees, combined with happy customers, provide the tangible returns that any organization wants: higher retention, higher productivity, and higher profits.

Starting with employees, it is important to help them not only have a great experience while they are working, but to understand the importance of providing a great customer experience. As we saw in the Chick-Fil-A example earlier, creating an environment where employees are prized can have real tangible outcomes for customers and profits.

It's very important to get this right *before* you start telling the world about how great you treat customers or employees. So, step 1 with people is to ensure you are providing a great work culture and environment. Step 2 is to align those people around treating customers well.

Process

It's great to have some customer and employee successes, but if you don't have a way to repeat those successes, you are going to be constantly fighting an uphill battle.

Process can be your ally in creating and maintaining great employee and customer experiences. For instance, if you put employee-centric and customer-centric goals within your processes you are already on your way towards success. This is where the governance property of the COX comes into play.

Platforms

As we talked about in both the (virtual) environments and platforms properties of the Center of Experience, the platform that underlies experience is a critical component.

Even the best people and processes with the most clearly defined goals can't achieve true success with experience unless they have the tools and technology to support them.

The best way to start here, however, is not by defining technologies and platforms to use, but rather by finding technologies that best suit the goals needed. This avoids the tendency of many organizations to build processes around existing technology products and solutions simply because they are too expensive and complex to modify. Technology should be used to support your experience goals, not the other way around!

Measures of Success

There's one more thing that will make the Center of Experience successful that falls slightly outside of the categories above, and that is tangible measures of success. It helps that the COX has measurement as one of its core components.

Additionally, I recommend you look at my book *Meaningful Measurement of the Customer Experience* (2022) for more ideas on measurement.

In the next few chapters, I'm going to go into more details about how to apply the ideas and components of the Center of Experience, starting with its experience maturity model.

Idea Starters

Similar to the ideas I shared in the last chapter which discussed some ways to get started with smaller approaches, the best way to be successful is to get both broad support across other teams within the company, as well as some measure of executive sponsorship.

Support from executive stakeholders will also generally signal that experience is a priority within the organization, and that they understand the direct link between employee satisfaction and customer satisfaction.

Getting these in place will ensure that your Center of Experience has a strong foundation and can withstand initial growing pains and the inevitable kinks that need to be worked out with any newer initiative.

3.2
The COX maturity model

I have worked with many types of organizations over the years to improve business results from experience and technology investments. While every organization that invests in experience wants to reap returns, how and where they start is dependent on their level of sophistication in a number of areas. Trying to undertake too complex an initiative could yield as bad of results as doing nothing at all, if the complex initiative is never able to truly get off the ground.

Thus, we need to assess a company's experience maturity level to determine the best and most realistic starting point. To that end, I have incorporated a experience maturity model to help organizations understand where they are in the experience journey and what needs to happen to accelerate getting better business results out of EX and CX initiatives.

Additionally, there are many existing maturity models, and your organization may already be using a different one. My advice here is to use common sense. If you have been consistently measuring your maturity using a different model, I think you should continue to use that one. If, however, you have not been measuring maturity already, the COX maturity model could work well.

Performing an experience maturity assessment at the beginning of an experience initiative ensures you are taking the right approaches across the different areas it measures. The assessment asks participating groups to rate an organization's maturity across different areas of both customer and employee experience. It's always an eye-opener to see the results of this assessment, as it can highlight things such as a clear weakness in a company, or even a lack of communication in certain areas where solutions exist but have not been widely shared.

I have provided a sample version of our initial maturity assessment (based on our proprietary and much longer maturity assessment we provide our clients) in Appendix 2 at the end of this book that you are welcome to use.

Let's explore the experience maturity model now in more detail.

The 5 stages of the maturity model

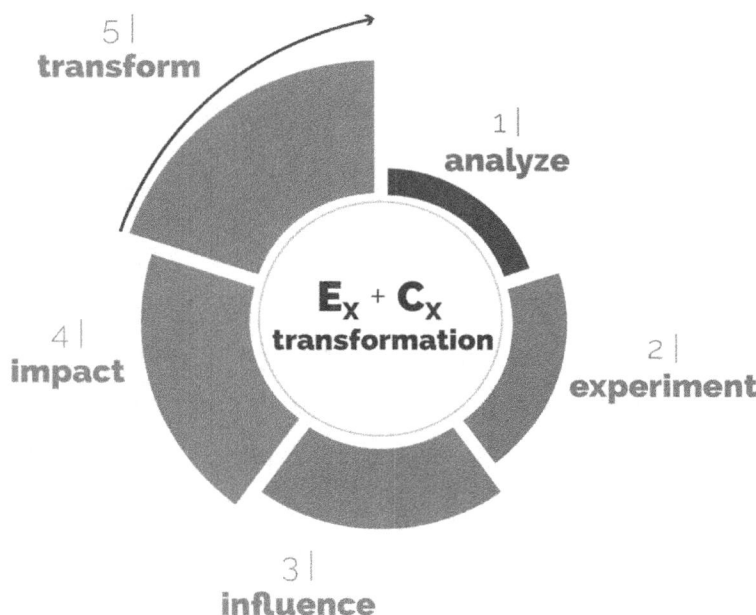

Figure 3.0: The Center of Experience maturity model

The improvement of a company's experience maturity is identified based on five stages that measure across both customer and employee experience:

Stage 1: Analyze

At this stage, an organization has functional competence, so is able to provide good products and services, but is only beginning to evaluate enhancing experience. Employees have the tools, environment, and technology to perform assigned tasks, but emphasis is not placed on their well-being or experience.

Customers are able to purchase products and services from the organization, and when successful, the experience is positive.
We can then look at the three primary categories of maturity as defined below:

- **Competence**
  There is functional competence within the organization in providing customers with good service, but teams and initiatives are siloed, and contributions or ROI are not immediately apparent. EX and CX are not embraced as keys to organizational success. When good employee experience or customer experience happens, it is not necessarily intentional.
- **Awareness**
  There is awareness within the organization that improved experience for both employees and customers could be beneficial but lack of consensus or understanding of how or where to start.
- **Action**
  CX and EX teams are taking ad hoc action, if any; there is a disconnect between experience team(s) and the rest of the organization, if any communication exists.

Stage 2: Experiment

At this second stage, an organization has begun trials to improve EX and CX. The organization begins to implement initiatives to engage employees with varying degrees of effectiveness. Experience and/or marketing teams are performing tests and optimizing portions of the customer experience.

- **Competence**

  At the experiment stage in maturity, there is activity related to innovation in both employee and customer experience, but there is not yet a cohesive strategy that ties this work together. In other words, customer experience initiatives and teams are having success in a silo, and so are employee experience teams, but the two are not connected in a meaningful way.

- **Awareness**

  At this stage, the organization has a clearer vision of how enhancing CX and EX can measurably improve key metrics in theory (or possibly in very small pilot projects), but it is not ready to commit large amounts of resources to do so. Experience enhancement initiatives are being created but have not made it to production yet.

- **Action**

  Proofs of concepts and trials are implemented. Experience team(s) and the rest of the organization are still disconnected.

Stage 3: Influence

In the influence stage, an organization is able to measure engagement from its employees and customers. Employees are provided with processes and methods to make their jobs easier and more satisfying. Interacting and buying from the organization is a positive experience, made easier by processes, environment and technology. Somewhere between stage 2 and 3 is where the "novice" customer experience organizations exist, which, according to a 2019 Hotjar CX survey, comprise about 40% of all companies[42]. Please note that this study only pertains to *customer* experience and not a combination of both CX and EX.

- **Competence**

  EX & CX initiatives are in effect, and are *influencing* decisions across the organization in a positive way, with visibility to stakeholders across the organization, and demonstrable measures of success.

  At this point, customer and employee experience have also been explicitly stated as being key to organizational success.

- **Awareness**

  At the influence stage in maturity, the organization has several successes with experience design improvement in production across different lines of business, practice areas and teams. There is increased focus on coordination and sharing of learning between teams.

- **Action**

  The organization is proactive in identifying experience-related issues; there is closer coordination between customer experience and employee experience teams and other parts of the organization.

Stage 4: Impact

At this fourth stage in the maturity model, an organization and their customers are starting to feel results in their investments. Employees are actively contributing and feel valued by their employer and satisfied with their work.

Customers feel rewarded and valued and become frequent customers, recommend to others, and post positive reviews. Between stages 3 and 4 is where that same Hotjar study would peg "competent" companies in CX, which comprise about 38% of all organizations.

- **Competence**
  At this stage, the organization has a good understanding of how investments in EX and CX can contribute to the bottom line based on some recent successes.

- **Awareness**
  The organization has a strategy to incorporate enhanced experience in its major initiatives, and has some incidental success with some experience improvements. There is an understanding that operational streamlining is required but lacking definition of it.
  We call this stage *impact* because stakeholders within the company are starting to see meaningful progress and returns from their investments in experience.

- **Action**
  Despite being proactive in identifying solutions, the organization is still mostly reactive in its solutions, and due to

lack of repeatable processes, the organization finds itself re-inventing approaches to improving experience, losing significant time in implementation and organization, high cost-to-benefit ratio.

Stage 5: Transform

In the final stage, an organization is actively integrating its CX and EX efforts for the growth of the organization. Employees are actively improving the company, and are able to collaborate with *customers* to improve their organization. Customers are actively involved in providing feedback and ideas to improve the company's products and services.

This is the area where the same Hotjar study would consider an organization to be "mature" in CX, which comprises only 12% of companies. Remember, this also doesn't include how both EX and CX are combined into Brand Experience. While there isn't a standardized measurement of that just yet, based on my experience, the percentages of mature and competent companies would be lower if both were factored together.

- **Competence**

  At the transform stage in maturity, the organization is reaping the benefits of EX and CX being priorities. Strategic initiatives include experience as a key component and design element.

- **Awareness**

  A sharp focus on employee and customer experience as a competitive advantage is embedded throughout the whole organization. The company is continuously looking for ways to further improve, expand and invest in processes, tooling, and skills.

- **Action**

  Continuous improvement is occurring across both customer and employee experience; teams are working together and there is alignment across CX and EX strategy, design, and implementation.

When an organization can align employee and customer experience and get to reach the Transform phase in all three categories, it truly starts to achieve Return on Experience (RO_X).

As we discussed previously under the measurement component section, this return can be seen through indicators such as an improvement in Net Promoter Score (NPS) from customers and Employee Net Promoter Score (eNPS) in employees, as well as more tangible results such as the following:

- Improved employee retention
- Improved employee productivity
- Increased customer loyalty
- Increased word of mouth referrals

The experience maturity model within the Center of Experience identifies ten elements that require an organization's attention. An organization needs to improve balance across these elements to deliver the accelerated transformation that unified EX & CX can deliver.

The 10 Elements of the experience maturity model

At each stage in the experience maturity model, we use specific categories to analyze and assess an organization's capabilities and maturity across the two primary areas that combine to make brand experience: customer experience and employee experience. Thus, we measure acceleration across the entire organization using the 10 elements of experience:

1. Strategy
2. Ideation
3. Cohesion
4. Process
5. Culture
6. Environment
7. Intelligence
8. Technology
9. Compliance
10. Results

For an organization to achieve true brand experience, they need to pay attention to the 10 identified elements of experience. For the best results, it requires a well-balanced approach across these elements. An organization which is very mature in one area but lacking on others, will face issues. As such it is important for organizations to understand which element(s) they are strongest and weakest at, in order to create a plan to improve each. This often involves focusing on weaker elements, while having a more gradual plan to improve the elements in which they are already strong.

This will allow organizations to recognize where their weaknesses and strengths are when it comes to implementing experience initiatives. While we don't cover all of the above in this book, we work with our clients to identify the relevant characteristics which come in unique variations for each organization.

I also acknowledge that some organizations are much more advanced in one area or another between customer and employee experience. Understanding the size of the gap between the maturity of CX and EX is another outcome of going through this exercise and can often help organizations determine where to focus some of their immediate efforts.

This means that the maturity measurement is a relative scale for each organization, based on several factors, including:

- Industry (factoring in competitors)
- Size (employees and revenue)
- Age (years in business)
- as well as a few other factors

To illustrate this point, let's go back to the Hotjar 2019 CX study I referenced earlier. If you look at the proportion of companies that ranked as "mature" versus "novice," there is a marked contrast between those with $500M+ in revenue and those below. Twenty-eight percent of mature companies were in that high revenue bracket, versus only 10% that were in the novice bracket.

Defining the 10 elements in the model

Let's now explore each of the elements in the experience maturity model in more depth:

Strategy

This refers to the executive/leadership's directions towards optimization of experience and how it maps to organizational priorities and objectives. The more mature an organization is, the more realistic expectations at the leadership level are in terms of return on investment (ROI) timeframes, the level of investment that is required, as well as the level of improvement that can be achieved.

Ideation

This is the process to identify, plan and socialize experience initiatives that provide business impact and return on investment (ROI). The ideal roadmap extends beyond single teams and envisions a company-wide effort to optimize experience across the enterprise. It is a continuous process supported by the right tools and the required organizational commitments.

Cohesion

This describes the way experience initiatives are embedded/integrated in the organizational structure. Areas include:

- Business Collaboration
- Organizational Structure
- Roles & Responsibilities

- Training

When experience optimization is prioritized across several business units it indicates a more mature organization. In addition to using more advanced techniques within a single unit, the organization is often addressing more complex and cross-functional needs. Rather than being relegated to a single department or use case, experience optimization can be utilized in cost reduction, revenue increase, HR, finance, legal/risk, and many other areas.

This allows each part of an organization to more fully understand its data and leverage it to make better decisions. It also allows these experience-driven businesses to use data to make better decisions across the entire organization.

Culture

Work culture should be approached as the operating system it really is. It is comprised of the explicit and implicit behaviors and expectations that shape the workforce. Part of achieving brand experience maturity involves understanding and optimizing the drivers of on-brand versus off-brand behavior.

Rather than focus on lagging indicators such as the results of ineffectual employee engagement surveys, a good experience practitioner sharpens their lens on leading indicators such as intrinsic motivators. This approach allows you to instantly map and "decode" what motivates the individual, a key building block to assembling a working Employee Experience (EX) model. Through cultural analytics tools, you can then map organization-wide behaviors that accelerate versus inhibit reaching business goals. From this process we are able to design meaningful action plans specifically tied to business objectives.

Keep in mind as well that although culture extends beyond employees, everything starts internally. Your employee culture will reflect outward to your customer culture. While they may not be the same, employee and customer culture are tied to one another. The same applies to partners and vendors.

Environment

The overall organizational environment must be one that is conducive to improvement. While this can be measured and managed in many ways, the physical (condition and design of employee and customer spaces), cultural, and digital environments must align to one that is designed to comprehensively enhance the experience of both employees and customers.

Organizations should also understand and embrace the need for virtual workspaces, whether those are remote workers, or as functionality such as augmented reality (AR) and virtual reality (VR) become more commonplace in work.

Intelligence

The future of work is a collaboration between people and artificial intelligence. How companies embrace this truth can often dictate their fate in the hands of competition that is rapidly adopting automation, machine learning, and other practices that heavily rely on data science.

Artificial intelligence and data science adoption and application provide a short-term competitive advantage and have longer-term benefits as the world moves toward a more automated workforce.

Technology

This is the technical foundation for experience, including the basis for the people, processes and technology to perform data science-related tasks and projects. Areas include:

- Infrastructure
- Data
- Integration (inputs, models, outputs)
- Supporting Tools

For an organization to mature with experience, there should be an IT *environment* and culture that supports making the improvement of experience for employees and customers as efficient as possible. This means access to the right tools and environments to train, as well as access to data and means to integrate AI models and other augmentations, even with business-critical applications. Of course, this has to be balanced with constraints in terms of security and costs.

Process

This refers to the process and procedures to initiate projects and provide results with experience optimization including:

- Preparation
- Modeling

- Testing
- Deployment
- Monitoring

Within this process, there is also a need for greater collaboration, and more mature organizations are already seeing the benefits here. When cross-functional teams are able to contribute to a continuous cycle of insights delivery, with reusable and shareable components utilized across the business, collaboration takes on a small, focused perspective as well as a broader, company-wide perspective.

This idea of collaboration extends to deployment as well. There is a stark difference in maturity between a company who simply embarks on siloed experience initiatives versus integrating these efforts with other programs throughout the business. Those businesses that augment decision-making with experience-driven solutions are able to move more quickly towards better results for both employees and customers. Process and methodology also refer to the way knowledge is captured and transcribed and includes things like IP protection and other related items.

Compliance

A comprehensive investment in experience requires ensuring legal and ethical compliance across a broad range of issues.

This includes addressing privacy concerns, such as those regulated by GDPR, or accessibility needs, as regulated by the U.S. Rehabilitation Act of 1975 (commonly referred to as "Section 508" after the part of the Act that deals with accessibility for the Web), or the Americans with Disabilities Act (ADA), including many other areas.

In particular industries and use cases, this also includes HIPAA compliance, to other privacy requirements needed when dealing with personally identifiable information (PII) or personal health information (PHI), and many other laws and guidelines.

When referring to the application of artificial intelligence and data science, this refers to the way technical risks are managed. For instance, artificial intelligence has unique needs which can include:

- Explainable
- Ethical
- Non-biased
- Reproducible
- Auditable
- Secure

Results

Finally, any investment in experience must be measured to determine its success. This is the way EX and CX initiatives are measured and evaluated from a business perspective, and how they are measured against key organizational performance goals.

A mature organization will tie experience to its KPIs, and measuring the return on investment in its experience initiatives. We refer to this measurement as the Return on Experience (RO_X).

Application of the experience maturity model

An organization that is investing in experience can use the Experience Maturity Model to guide its journey toward receiving true RO_x. The Center of Experience uses this model to assess an organization and determine the best and most appropriate course of action to take it successfully from its current state to the optimal "Transform" state, or the 5th stage in the model. Organizations receive a "report card" that visualizes where they are in overall maturity as well as maturity according to the 10 elements.

In addition to assessing where an organization currently stands, the assessment also identifies industry or competitor benchmarks as well as company targets along each of the elements.

This assessment is then used to help a company improve these individual aspects, often with a customized, agile-sprint-based plan to bring the organization to the next level of acceleration. This collaborative approach allows teams within the organization to contribute ideas and work to accelerate the organization's experience initiatives.

Idea starter

My suggestion to get started is actually contained within this book. Use the experience maturity model initial assessment for your organization to see where you are. Give it to your team, or at least a few others in your organization to get a broader set of data.

Conclusion

Thanks for joining me on this journey, and I hope that the experience (pun intended) was worthwhile. The Center of Experience framework provides a lot of guidance and areas to consider, but ultimately it is up to you and your team to implement what makes sense for your organization.

Thus, even more important than any of the details shared in the previous pages is the ultimate premise, that motivated employees who understand the purpose of their work create healthy organizational cultures which are aligned according to common goals, and provide customers with great experiences that they return for and tell others about.

How the Center of Experience Works

Let's revisit the diagram of the entire COX from earlier (Figure 4.1). The diagram shows all of the working parts of the Center of Experience that we've spent the previous pages discussing.

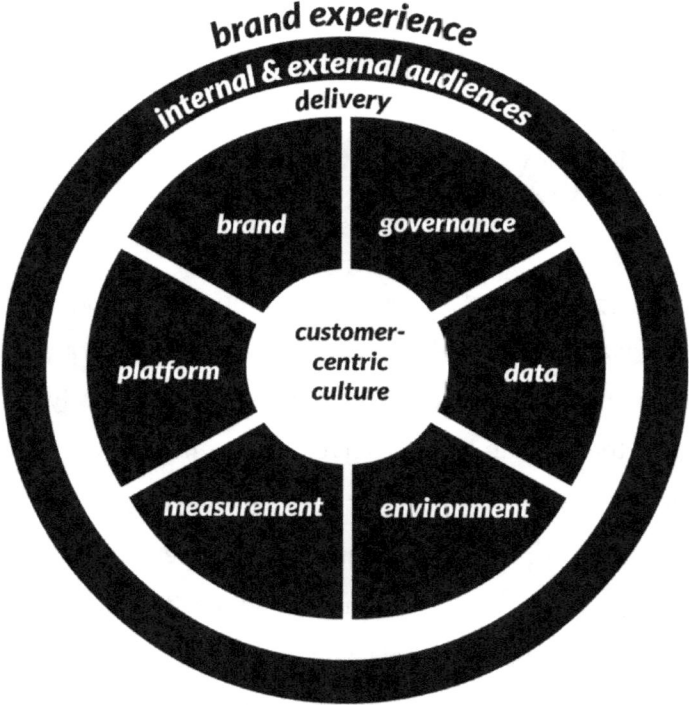

Figure 4.1, The Center of Experience Model

Implementing the Center of Experience requires that all these elements are addressed in a meaningful way, as we've outlined in the previous chapters. Whether by internal or external teams, or a combination of both, to be most successful means that all parts are working together. It also means that both the EX and CX components are addressed, measured and optimized over time.

The Center of Experience offers any organization the ability to truly effect change and become an experience-led organization. The benefits are numerous, including employee retention and increased productivity, as well as greater customer satisfaction which translates to increased sales.

Final Thoughts

Brand experience is the sum of *every* experience that *every* leader, employee, customer, partner and vendor has with that brand. If that sounds overwhelming, it doesn't have to be. Just as this book outlines the individual parts of the Center of Experience, creating a brand experience for your organization needs to start with individual pieces. It is also important to make sure that you have a team which is aligned in the belief that investments in experience (both CX and EX) are worth the time and effort.

My hope is that you can apply the principles and methodologies behind the Center of Experience in your own organization. Good luck and I'd love to hear about your own experiences!

Appendix 1:
Glossary

Brand Experience:

The combination of customer experience (CX) and employee experience (EX), and how both work together to form an organization's holistic experience and brand perception.

Center of Excellence:

For this, I'm going to reference Pega's excellent definition here[43]:

A Center of Excellence (COE) is at heart a group of people – experts in business process management, customer relationship management, and business domain, equipped with an arsenal of best practices and tools. A mature COE is a self-directing entity responsible for supporting business users and shepherding complex projects to successful completion."

Center of Experience (COX)

A Center of Excellence that is built around promoting brand experience, or the combination of employee and customer experience. It is a multi-disciplinary group of teams and experts with the ability to create projects and initiatives to improve CX and EX.

Culture Gap

This is the difference, or "gap" between three things as measured using the culture quadrant:

- What employees *perceive* the current culture to be
- What employees *desire* the culture to be
- What leadership and stakeholders desire the culture to be in order to achieve business objectives

Culture Quadrant

Based on the original academic research done to produce the Competing Values Framework (CVF), the Center of Experience's Culture Quadrant consists of four primary areas which help define the dominant characteristics of a company culture: collaboration, creation, competition, and control. No company is solely one of these but a combination of varying degrees of each.

Customer Experience (CX)

This is the sum of all interactions a customer has with a brand throughout the customer journey, from pre-sale, during the sale, and after the sale. Customer Experience is one of the primary points of competition for a majority of brands today.

Employee Experience (EX)

This is the sum of all interactions an employee has with their employer, throughout the employee journey, from recruiting and hiring, to their transition out of the company. Employee Experience involves many disciplines and roles within an organization to be successful, from HR to technology and more.

Experience Maturity

This is the measurement of how advanced an organization's employee and customer experience processes, methods, and tools are. The Center of Experience contains a maturity model that allows an organization to assess how sophisticated, documented, understood, and repeatable its customer and employee experience practices are.

A sample initial maturity assessment is provided in Appendix B of this book.

Extrinsic Motivation

This refers to items used to inspire and motivate employees to be more productive and stay at a company longer, which include external rewards or outcomes. These are things like money (salary increases, bonuses, etc.) or perks (free lunches, foosball tables, etc.).

While extrinsic motivation can have a positive effect for short periods of time and for limited activities and roles, it is widely agreed that their effect not only diminishes over time but can actually work to diminish employee motivation.

Intrinsic Motivation

This refers to items used to inspire and motivate employees to be more productive and increase their tenure, which appeal to the intrinsic nature of human beings.

Unlike extrinsic motivators, these intrinsic ones are more fundamental to an individual and their effects do not diminish with time as long as they are properly addressed. The amount of intrinsic motivation in relation to the potential for an employee to be motivated is measured using the motivator gap.

Next Best Action

This is a more dynamic method to orchestrating an employee or customer's experience, as it takes a user-centered approach to determine exactly what a buyer wants, and not necessarily what a seller hopes they will do.

It takes into account a number of different factors, such as a person's demographics, past actions and behaviors, and other criteria unique to an individual, and then determines what the next step should be in order to drive the buyer to a desired behavior.

Appendix 2:
Experience Maturity Assessment Sample

The following is an example of an experience maturity assessment that I have used with clients across many industries. You are welcome to use this either as is, or make some modifications to it.

To calculate maturity, you simply calculate the score for each main category (the items in the left column, e.g. Strategy, Ideation, etc.)

	Strategy	How extensively are the following integrated into enterprise-wide strategy?
		Rate from 1 (lowest) to 5 (highest)
		Customer Experience:
		Employee Experience:
		How equally are the following integrated into organization's strategic Key

	Performance Indicators (KPIs) and other business goals:
	Rate from 1 (lowest) to 5 (highest)
	Customer Experience:
	Employee Experience:
Ideation	**How clear is the organizational roadmap for optimizing:**
	Rate from 1 (lowest) to 5 (highest)
	Customer Experience: .
	Employee Experience:
	How inclusive is the experience roadmap of all facets of CX or EX in the organization, as well as all departments involved?
	Rate from 1 (lowest) to 5 (highest)
	Customer Experience:
	Employee Experience:
Cohesion	**How successfully are the different divisions, departments, etc. of your organization able to work together to implement initiatives that improve:**
	Rate from 1 (lowest) to 5 (highest)
	Customer Experience:
	Employee Experience:
	How aligned are customer experience and employee experience goals and initiatives with one another within the organization?

	Rate from 1 (lowest) to 5 (highest)
	Customer Experience:
	Employee Experience:
Culture	**How aligned is the organizational culture to improving:**
	Rate from 1 (lowest) to 5 (highest)
	Customer Experience:
	Employee Experience:
	How fragmented are individual roles and responsibilities in their ability to address enterprise-wide experience challenges?
	Rate from 1 (lowest) to 5 (highest)
	Customer Experience:
	Employee Experience:
Environment	**How extensively are physical environments designed and optimized around customer and employee needs (vs. internal constraints)?**
	Rate from 1 (lowest) to 5 (highest)
	Customer Experience:
	Employee Experience:
	How extensively are virtual environments designed and optimized around customer and employee needs (vs. internal constraints)?
	Rate from 1 (lowest) to 5 (highest)

	Customer Experience:
	Employee Experience:
Intelligence	How effectively does your organization utilize data science to tie together elements of the employee and customer journey?
	Rate from 1 (lowest) to 5 (highest)
	Customer Experience:
	Employee Experience:
	How deep a role does data science and analytics play in planning and optimizing your experience initiatives?
	Rate from 1 (lowest) to 5 (highest)
	Customer Experience:
	Employee Experience:
Technology	Are your customer- and employee -facing technology platforms assessed and designed with the user in mind (vs. organizational hierarchy and constraints)?
	Rate from 1 (lowest) to 5 (highest)
	Customer Experience:
	Employee Experience:
	How streamlined are the applications and technology platforms that power experience?

	Rate from 1 (lowest) to 5 (highest)
	Customer Experience:
	Employee Experience:
Process	**How well-documented are the processes and systems related to:**
	Rate from 1 (lowest) to 5 (highest)
	Customer Experience:
	Employee Experience:
	How extensively are experience-related processes and systems reviewed to optimize and improve them?
	Rate from 1 (lowest) to 5 (highest)
	Customer Experience:
	Employee Experience:
Results	**How extensively is experience being measured, and is their performance tied to KPIs for the organization?**
	Rate from 1 (lowest) to 5 (highest)
	Customer Experience:
	Employee Experience:
	Are business leaders seeing quantifiable results from their investments in customer and employee experience?
	Rate from 1 (lowest) to 5 (highest)
	Customer Experience:

	Employee Experience:
Compliance	**How regularly are the following processes reviewed for compliance with both internal and external standards and regulations:**
	Rate from 1 (lowest) to 5 (highest)
	Customer Experience:
	Employee Experience:
	Does the organization have a transparent, ethical, and compliant way to ensure there is an equally positive experience for all:
	Rate from 1 (lowest) to 5 (highest)
	Customer Experience:
	Employee Experience:

Experience Maturity Score

To calculate the Experience Maturity Score, add up the totals for each item under the appropriate category (CX or EX) and place it in the "Total Sum" field. Then, to find the average, divide the total by the number of questions per type (e.g. 20 for CX and EX, or 40 for Brand Experience).

Type	Total Sum	Maturity Score (Average)
Customer Experience		

	Employee Experience		
EX)	Brand Experience (CX +		

If you'd like more detail, add up the totals and find the Experience Maturity Score for each of the 10 categories. That will give you insight on more specific gaps that your organization might have.

About the Author

Greg Kihlström is a best-selling author, speaker, and entrepreneur, currently an advisor and consultant to top companies on marketing technology, customer experience, and digital transformation initiatives as Principal and Chief Strategist at GK5A. He is also the host of The Agile Brand with Greg Kihlström podcast. He is a two-time CEO and co-founder, growing both companies organically and through acquisitions and ultimately leading both to be acquired (one in 2017 and the other in 2021). He has worked with some of the world's top brands, including Adidas, Choice Hotels, Coca-Cola, Dell, FedEx, HP, Marriott, MTV, Starbucks, Toyota, and VMware.

He earned his MBA from Quantic School of Business and Technology and is a member of the School of Marketing Faculty at the Association of National Advertisers. He currently serves on the University of Richmond's Customer Experience Advisory Board and the Workhouse Arts Foundation Board as chair of the Marketing Committee. Greg was the founding chair of the American Advertising Federation's National Innovation Committee and served on the

Virginia Tech Pamplin College of Business Marketing Mentorship Advisory Board. Greg is Lean Six Sigma Black Belt certified, is a Certified Agile Coach (ICP-ACC) and holds a certification in Business Agility (ICP-BAF).

Greg has had multiple internationally best-selling books, including his Agile Brand Guides series on marketing technology platforms and practices. His eleventh and most recent book, *House of the Customer* (2023), discusses the 1:1 personalized customer experience of the future and how brands can organize the people, processes, and platforms that enable it. *Meaningful Measurement of the Customer Experience* (2022) provides guidance on creating a customer-centric culture that prioritizes customer needs while aligning internal teams around a common goal. His award-winning podcast, "The Agile Brand with Greg Kihlström," launched in early 2019, discusses brand strategy, marketing, and customer experience with some of the world's leading experts and leaders.

Greg is a contributing writer to Fast Company, Forbes, MarTech, and CMSWire, and has been featured in publications such as Advertising Age and The Washington Post. Greg has been named a 2022 Top 10 Marketing and Customer Experience Thought Leader by Thinkers 360, was named one of ICMI's Top 25 CX Thought Leaders two years in a row, and a DC Inno 50 on Fire as a DC trendsetter in Marketing. He's participated as a keynote speaker and panelist at industry events worldwide, including Internet Week New York, Internet Summit, DigiMarCon, Digital Summit, EventTech, MarTech, SMX Social Media, and VMworld. He has guest lectured at several colleges and universities, including VCU Brandcenter, Georgetown University, Duke University, American University, University of Maryland, Howard University, and Virginia Tech.

Greg lives in Alexandria, Virginia, with his wife, Lindsey.

References

[1] Wiles, Jackie. "Gartner Top 3 Priorities for HR Leaders in 2019." Gartner. December 12, 2018.

[2] https://www.pwc.com/us/en/advisory-services/publications/consumer-intelligence-series/pwc-consumer-intelligence-series-customer-experience.pdf

[3] Deloitte, Duke University Fuqua School of Business, American Marketing Association. The CMO Survey. August 2019.

[4] Morgan, Blake. "The Un-Ignorable Link Between Employee Experience and Customer Experience." *Forbes*. February 2018.

[5] https://www.gallup.com/workplace/349484/state-of-the-global-workplace-2022-report.aspx

[6] Sorofman, Jake. "Gartner Surveys Confirm Customer Experience is the New Battlefield." Gartner. October 23, 2014.

[7] Pemberton, Chris. "Key Findings From the Gartner Customer Experience Survey." Gartner. March 16, 2018.

[8] Loucks, Jeff, Tom Davenport, and David Schatsky. "State of AI in the Enterprise, 2nd Edition." *Deloitte Insights*. October 2018.

[9] Qualtrics. "Employee Engagement Benchmark Study, 2017." 2017.

[10] Berkeley Executive Education. "Culture as a Powerful Leadership Tool." Executive.Berkeley.edu.

[11] Grant Thornton and Oxford Economics. "Return on Culture: Proving the Connection Between Culture and Profit" 2019.

[12] Birkner, Christine. "How Treating Employees Well Boosts Brand Value." *Adweek.* May 17, 2016.

[13] Howard, Larry W. "Validating the Competing Values Model as a Representation of Organizational Cultures." *The International Journal of Organizational Analysis.* March 1, 1998.

[14] Grant Thornton and Oxford Economics. "Return on Culture: Proving the connection between culture and profit" 2019.

[15] Quinn, R. E. and J. Rohrbaugh. (1983). A Spatial Model of Effectiveness Criteria: Towards a Competing Values Approach to Organizational Analysis. *Management Science*, 29(3), 363-377.

[16] Wallach EJ (1983) "Individuals and organizations: The cultural match." Train Dev J 37: 28–36.

[17] Cameron KS, Quinn RE (2006) *Diagnosing and changing organizational culture: Based on the Competing Values Framework.* San Francisco, CA: Jossey-Bass.

[18] Martin J, Meyerson D (1988) "Organizational cultures and the denial, channeling and acknowledgement of ambiguity." In: L R Pondy, R J Boland and H Thomas, editors. *Managing Ambiguity and Change.* Chichester, England: John Wiley and Sons.

[19] Cameron KS, Quinn RE (1999) *Diagnosing and Changing Organizational Culture: Based on the Competing Values Framework.* Reading, MA: Addison-Wesley.

[20] Brown, Karen. "To Retain Employees, Focus on Inclusion—Not Just Diversity." *Harvard Business Review.* December 4, 2018.

[21] Microsoft and ConStat Inc. Microsoft Office Personal Productivity Challenge. January 2005.

[22] Keith, Elise. "55 Million: A Fresh Look at the Number, Effectiveness, and Cost of Meetings in the U.S." *Lucid Meeetings.* December 4, 2015.

[23] Rosenbloom, Stephanie (August 7, 2010). "But Will It Make You Happy?". *The New York Times.* Retrieved August 16, 2010.

[24] Gallup. State of the American Workforce. 2017.

[25] https://www.gallup.com/workplace/349484/state-of-the-global-workplace.aspx
1.   "CX stats and trends," Hotjar, accessed October 18, 2022.
       https://www.hotjar.com/customer-experience/trends-and-stats/

[27] Gallup. State of the American Workplace. 2017.
https://www.gallup.com/workplace/238085/state-american-workplace-report-2017.aspx

[28] Harvard Management Update. "Rapid Onboarding at Capital One." *Harvard Business Review*. February 27, 2008.

[29] Clifford, Catherine. "The Founder of Patagonia Fishes Half the Year and Tells His Employees to Go Surfing." CNBC. December 2016.

[30] Kohll, Alan. "How Your Office Space Effects Impacts Employee Well-Being." *Forbes*. January 24, 2019.

[31] World Green Building Council. "Health, Wellbeing, & Productivity in Offices: The Next Chapter for Green Building." September 2014.

[32] 2013 U.S. Workplace Survey. Gensler.

[33] Lars Foldspang, Michael Mark, Louise Lund Rants, Laurits Rømer Hjorth, Christian Langholz-Carstensen, Otto Melchior Poulsen, Ulf Johansson, Guy Ahonen and Steinar Aasnæss (TemaNord). "Working environment and productivity: A register-based analysis of Nordic enterprises." 2014

[34] Deloitte, Duke University Fuqua School of Business, American Marketing Association. CMO Survey. August 2019.

[35] Borysenko, Karlyn. "What Was Management Thinking? The High Cost of Employee Turnover." TLNT. April 22, 2015.

[36] Reilly, Robyn. "Five Ways to Improve Employee Engagement Now." Gallup. 2016.

[37] McCreary, Matthew. "Chick-fil-A Makes More Per Restaurant Than McDonald's, Starbucks and Subway Combined...and It's Closed on Sundays." *Entrepreneur*. 2019.

[38] Epsilon. New Epsilon Research Indicates 80% of Consumers are More Likely to Make a Purchase When Brands Offer Personalized Experiences." Epsilon.com. January 9, 2018.

[39] Economist Intelligence Unit (EIU). "Mobility, Performance, and Engagement." 2016"

[40] Samsung. "Maximizing Mobile Value: Is BYOD Holding You Back?" June 2018

[41] IT Pro Portal. "Why BYOD in the Workplace Increases Productivity." December 22, 2015.

[42] Hotjar. "CX Trends for 2019." October 11, 2019.

---

[43] Pega. "What is a COE?" https://www.pega.com/services/consulting/centers-of-excellence– retrieved November 15, 2019